QUINZEL'S GUIDE TO LIFE

A COLLECTION OF ARTICLES TOLD BY AN EVERYDAY GEEKY GIRL

QUINZEL LEE

Rose Gold Press, LLC
Chicago, Illinois
www.RoseGoldPress.com

Paperback ISBN: 978-1-7354167-8-6

Developmental Editor:
Rhonda Merwath
Rhonda Edits

Copy Editor/Proofreading:
Paulette Nunlee
5-Star Proofing

Cover Design:
Sherelle Green

QUINZEL'S GUIDE TO LIFE

Quinzel's Guide to Life is a collection of articles told by an everyday geeky girl.

Hi! My name is Quinzel. You don't know me, but I am someone that you already know. I am the weird child in your elementary class who gets excited about the stars, planets, and writing papers over the weekend. I am the pre-teen girl who took a book to read at the school dance. I am that girl that falls a little too hard for guys.

In this collection, I share the many ups and downs I've faced in life, sarcastic memes, a sex toy review that had me cackling as I was writing it and so much more.

If you are that awkward oddball, who doesn't quite fit in and gets excited about all of the little things... Welcome!

I hope you brought snacks. We're going to be here for a while.

To my amazing and loving husband
There, I wrote the damn book. Are you happy now?

INTRODUCTION
I AM SOMEONE YOU ALREADY KNOW

My name is Quinzel. You don't know me, but I am someone that you already know.

I am the weird child in your elementary school who gets excited about the stars and planets and writing papers over the weekend. It's true. As a kid, I'd often get into trouble for filling up all of the extra notebooks at home with my random stories.

Seventy-page wide-ruled notebook? Little Quinzel was coming for you.

I am that even weirder child who couldn't be traditionally punished. Often sent to the computer room for talking out of turn, those huge, hefty black and green monitor screens fascinated me. Pages and pages of stories were printed off on a dot matrix printer. Eager to share my story, I was just as excited to tear off the edges of the paper. After spending a timeout in the computer room, I can still see the shock and disappointment as I handed my teacher a forty-page story I'd printed off. She had hoped— I think—I would spend the time reflecting upon my

punishment, not finding another way to talk excessively—
just through writing.

I am the pre-teen girl who carried a book to read to the
school dance. Look! I am not even going to bore you with
the details of my "middle school was awkward" phase. Just
know that I repeatedly flipped back and forth between
trying to be cool and "screw you, you think I'm weird
anyway."

I was the girl crying under the stairway at school who
you don't know what to say to her. This would follow me
through the rest of my life. The random bursts of tears.
Not really knowing why I'm crying. Well into my adult
years, I learned that therapy is one heck of a solution.

I am that kid who's a little too into (insert fandom
here). I didn't have therapy when I was younger. What I
had at my disposal was bands and TV shows. My entire
fantasy world was built of what my life would be like
involving those things. Every Tuesday, my TV was domi-
nated by a vampire slayer, and I would have done everything to be JUST like her.

I am that girl who falls a little TOO hard for guys. I
wanted a love like Buffy and Angel. Now, as an adult, I
totally get why that's not even practical in the least. I'd say
there was a part of me that still wanted that in adulthood,
maybe not the vampire part so much, but that once in a
lifetime, passionate, spark-inducing love.

I am the woman in your office wearing her Wonder
Woman shirt under her blazer.

I'm unbothered by the "isn't gaming for kids?"
comments because...well, I like kids. They're sweet, they're
honest, and they aren't stressed out about bills. Being free
and childlike is what I aspire to be.

I am every black woman who's been called a "white"
girl. Talking properly and watching anything besides BET

got me the label early on in life. Anyway, what's up with that? Never mind. I know the answer. The crazy thing is growing up I assumed I was the only one who had endured such remarks. That I was the only one who stood out. But it took going to college several states away to realize that with my quirks, my weirdness… I was NOT alone.

The weird thing? This brought me to meeting Leslie, and eventually, writing for *Geeky Girls Guide to Life*.

Leslie and I were in the same online black nerd group. Black women just nerding out about so many things. She made a post about looking to see if anyone wanted to write for her blog *Geeky Girl's Guide to Life*. I commented "SOLD." We worked great together. I nervously sent her blog posts to approve and she happily did.

One particular moment that made me cry tears of joy was when she sent me business cards that read "Quinzel Lee, Community and Content Manager."

I couldn't understand how she could give me so much trust and so much praise.

"Easy," she told me once, "I already know you."

My journey to write for *Geeky Girl's Guide to Life* has been an incredible adventure. I've shown up with my fair share of ups and downs, sarcastic memes, and a sex toy review that had me cackling while writing. You may have never heard of me or read my blog, but I know you've met someone like me before.

And if you are that person who's the oddball in your group, who doesn't quite fit in, who gets excited about all of the little things…

Hi, my name is Quinzel. Welcome! I hope you brought snacks. We're going to be here for a while.

THE BIRTH OF A GEEK

CHAPTER ONE

NERDING OUT WITH QUINZEL: QUINZEL'S QUIRK CABIN

I f someone were to slap a warning label on you, what would it say? For me, I'd imagine one of those black and white parental advisory stickers with the words "I'm Weird" written across my forehead.

I don't have an explosive temper. Never really even had a colorful past. The more normal you consider yourself, the weirder your perception of me.

Being weird was like a curse in my early days. The way I talked, the things I read. The things that set my heart on fire were so different than my peers.

As a child, I lived in a low-income apartment complex. If I close my eyes, I can still see the detailing of the brick buildings. There was always a bit of a light haze of smoke in the air. There wasn't much upkeep in the landscaping of the buildings. I remember the bushes, mixed with brown and green. They felt stiff and prickly, almost like plastic. There was rarely ever any extended amount of time when it was quiet in the complex; people often talked so loud that you just ended up tuning it out. Quite honestly, when things got quiet was when you felt suspicious of your surroundings and panic would set in. Police sirens were as common a sound as a train whistle, it was just background noise to me.

Even before I attended school, the people around me knew, and also treated me, as if I was different. I hated this. I struggled with learning what people wanted me to say and how they expected me to act at such a young age. Looking back, my differences weren't as large as they painted. Sure, I had different interests and a way about me, but I was still human, with the same hopes and dreams and fears as everyone else. Still, I just sort of stood out. In the midst of the families yelling at each other in the apartment upstairs, I was happily singing to myself about fairy tales. I carried myself as if the world around me did not exist. And as you can imagine, that pissed a lot of people off.

Baby Quinzel didn't realize that people being pissed off at me for being myself was all about them and not about me. It would take a multitude of failed attempts at being something I'm not to fully embrace who I was.

Let's talk fandom, one of the first things that made me realize "shit, I am a huge geek!"

It all started…well, I'm not even sure how I got into it. There would be no way that anyone who I was around or lived with would have told me about *Buffy the Vampire Slayer*. All I know is I tuned in one Tuesday evening and was hooked.

This was not just an entry into geekery and fandom. *Buffy the Vampire Slayer* was something that taught me how to cope with really tough shit. *Buffy* made me feel like I can be a hero and was the first person to teach me I was not weak and could survive anything.

Keeping *Buffy* in my life proved to be very difficult. Black Baptist Christians typically frown upon anything that's considered different. Secular or worldly things were forbidden. You can bet a show about vampires that included witchcraft was enough to send them over the edge.

One of my uncles was flabbergasted when I rented the *Buffy The Vampire Slayer* video game on Xbox 360 (I'm dating myself here). There was a scene where the character Willow was levitating above a table. My uncle immediately snatched the game out of the console and scolded me for misleading him in renting a game featuring witchcraft.

If you knew how physically abusive he was, you would also be a little bit confused on how levitation got him so angry, but I digress.

Buffy was something that I had to hide from everyone, but something that saved me. I looked forward to watching every week. I can't tell you how hard it was to be the weird black girl and how many nights I spent crying over it. I didn't understand why I couldn't just be like everyone else.

I tried, and quickly failed, to blend in. Sounding cooler, using slang, less excitement. And as I just stated, it almost instantly failed every time. People could smell the fraud in me, as if I had "geek" tattooed on my forehead. My efforts shifted to selling others on my nerd life. If I could just show how cool this life was, then surely they would want to know more. But that quickly fizzled as well. No one wanted to voluntarily be labeled *The Weird Kid*.

The real reason I struggled to fit in so much was because I was never destined to be like everyone else. I was destined to be different.

Sometimes, I wish I could sit with twelve-year-old Quinzel, watch an episode of *Buffy the Vampire Slayer* with her, and tell her that everything is going to be okay. That she wasn't the only black person obsessed with vampire slayers and comic books. And that one day, the great things she did would make even *Buffy* proud.

Buffy the Vampire Slayer was also a huge icon for me because it got me into writing more. By now, we know that people write fanfiction. But back then, I didn't know what it was called, I just wrote. I wrote new stories about Buffy and the Scooby Gang and these stories were the bridge that helped me get through life, week by week. If I didn't have a new episode of *Buffy the Vampire Slayer*, I had my writing. Notebooks filled with penciled out *Buffy* stories that turned into poems about other things, turned into all out books.

The more I wrote, the better I felt about being weird. Being a writer gave a purpose to my weirdness.

Throughout the years I got older and focused on more fandoms. Before I accepted myself for who I was, I spent so much time—too much in fact—trying to gauge if I could show off who I really am. The first day of college was great—a time of such freedom and so much over-thinking. With every new person I met, I thought, *Do I tell them? Do I pretend to like what they like? Do I just nod so I don't talk too much?* If there is one thing I want to convey in this book, it's how much I wish I hadn't wasted that time thinking about it.

Wasted time trying to fit in. Caring so much of what someone would think of me. It wasn't until I learned to let go, to allow myself to enjoy the things I love, that I could experience life to the fullest.

And that feeling? Better than someone thinking you're cool. So much better than someone finding you acceptable enough to fade into the background with them.

You don't want to do that, geeky girl, you were born to stand out.

Who I am isn't even easily contained into one thing. It is a multitude of things crammed into one, very short human being. Ladies and gentlemen, I'd like to introduce to you: *Quinzel's Quirk Cabin*.

This is the best way to describe myself because I'm one big house of geekiness, divided into three separate rooms of just how geeky:

- Binge Watching TV Shows geek room.
- Words I Randomly Learned By Just Reading The Dictionary for Hours geek room.
- Daydreaming the Weirdest Scenarios Based on What I Just Watched On TV geek room.

Really, we all have our little quirk cabins. Some of us choose to lock those rooms away, while the rest of us leave those doors wide open, ready to cram in more quirks. I'm many things and you're many things. Let's look into how I rolled up into one big geek with some articles from *Geeky Girl's Guide to Life*.

CHAPTER TWO

GEEKIN' OUT WITH GEEKY SEX TOYS

C W: NSFW content including talks of masturbation and female anatomy. I also say the f-word because, well, I felt it was fucking appropriate considering the subject manner.

Geeky Sex Toys was kind enough to send me the toy in exchange for an honest review. In short, they were like, "masturbate with our product and talk about it openly and honestly." You can see why I couldn't turn that down.

I'm going to be straightforward for a second. Sex is healthy. Masturbation is healthy. Neither is gross or shameful.

Now that you are fully aware of my thoughts beforehand, you'll understand how un-shy (new word, I'm calling it) I am when it comes to sex toys.

But g e e k y sex toys?? You have my complete attention. One look around the Geeky Sex Toys site and it will have you geeking out from head to...yeah, that too. Emma and Josh, founders of Geeky Sex Toys are in Brisbane, Australia. They create, design, and make all of their toys BY HAND.

This duo of sex toy makers are no strangers to

fandoms either. With a clever use of puns, they've got lines such as Doctor Screw (the *Doctor Who Toy*), DickPool (the *Deadpool Toy*), Orgasms of the Galaxy (*Guardians of the Galaxy Toy*) and The Indulgers (yes, of course, it's *the Avengers Toy*).

I'm so excited to tell you all which toy I got the chance to review. Ladies and Gents, I give you, the <u>Dildek.</u>

The Dildek is, obviously, from the Doctor Screw collection. Modeled after the famous Daleks, I promise you it won't kill you. This one comes in two colors: black and gold and two sizes: large and small. The one I received is a small.

&

<u>Foreplay and First Impressions</u>

Upon opening the box, I was quite impressed. Pretty amazing handiwork. Honestly!

You know how you might see a really cool toy at a bachelorette party, but after actually examining it, realize it's just plastic crap? With something as cool as Doctor Who, I expected it might be lacking in quality and using the fandom to make up for it. I was proven wrong right on the spot. Visually, it looked exactly like the picture, there was no variation at all. The color was vibrant, not faded in anyway (I had the, gold one) and the design consistent throughout. If you're a nerd for consistency, say if the dots are all aligned correctly, they are. The craftmanship gets a 10/10.

So now I know it LOOKS good, my next thought is to see how long it would stay that way. I felt it was time to put this thing through a series of non-masturbation tests. These tests were mainly me throwing it as far as I could across the room, shaking it as hard as I could, and smacking it upside a couple different surfaces in my home.

The most awesome thing I discovered while playing around with the durability of this toy is that the bottom is actually a suction so that you can ride it, no partner needed. Slapping it on my kitchen floor and kicking it a little with my foot, I tested to see if it would stay. It did. With all this shaking and throwing, it did not create any tears in the silicone. Damn, this amazing grade of silicone! Damn, this amazing craftmanship! It's really hanging in there!

Now that I have hazed the shit out of it, it's time to get down to business.

Fuck and Fuckability by Quinzel Austen
    (Sorry, Jane Austen)

After being quite impressed with how well it handled several stress tests (okay I was mainly having fun), I needed to know about the Dildek's level of fuckability because...well, that's the whole reason I bought it, right?

As I stated earlier in the review, the Dildek comes in two sizes, large and small. While there's no shame in having dildos that are Hulk-sized, I was a bit intimidated by a large, so I requested a small.

Now, small does not mean slim. When I saw the size, I was *still* intimidated. *Like all of that needs to go into all of me?* So, if you are into slimmer sex toys, lube up.

Also, if you have small hands like me, you may benefit from a small instead of a large. It was only a slight challenge to hold on to. The bumpy texture definitely assists with having a good grip, even with lube applied. However, closer to the end is a wider base, so a little difficult to get a really good grip in. But, as an alternative, there is an option to use the base on a flat surface and ride, hands-free.

Size aside, the silicone feels great. I'd say it's skin-like, but I don't know if I've ever felt skin this good. It's perfectly smooth enough to move outside and inside of a vagina that makes you kind of forget that you're masturbating with a fandom toy.

Another nice thing about the Dildek is the bumpy texture. If you can get it just right, it makes great for clitoral stimulation. For me, it was easier to achieve by hand than by riding, since the bumps are closer to the bottom of the base.

The biggest challenge with the Dildek? Trying to stop making Doctor Who references during sex, but maybe you do this anyway. *Guilty*

. . .

Would I Recommend?

The quality of this toy is beyond impressive. It's durable, flexible, and downright cute.

I will level with you and tell you Geeky Sex Toys will cost you a pretty penny, but they are so worth the money.

10/10 would recommend you save up your coin and buy from them.

10/10 would cum again.

CHAPTER THREE

WHY YOU SHOULD ABSOLUTELY LIVE THE WAY KID FURY DOES

I f you don't know who Kid Fury is, you need to stop what you're doing right now and listen to *The Read* Podcast. Not only a certified geek, Kid Fury is someone who takes no shit. And, dammit, we should all be like him.

There's a segment in the podcast known as "Listener Letters" where people write in to get advice, usually on their relationship. While Kid Fury's tried and true advice is to "break up with him," you can't help but know that he's right. Every. Single. Time.

And he's not even just saying that to be funny. You can tell that he adheres to the advice he gives. Don't waste time with someone who won't treat you right, don't care what people think of you, and for the love of Pete, stand up for yourself.

So now you know why you should live your life this way:

Get a Dog

- Or a cat, or a turtle. Really any kind of animal you can love on. Okay good, but seriously, Kid Fury has this cute little dog named Link and she even has her own Instagram. The guys you date may be crappy, but pets are awesome.

Get into Therapy

- I love a person who is an advocate for therapy. Because you can't get to a place where you don't have time to deal with fuckboys if you don't first take a look inside of yourself. He openly admits that he goes to therapy and you can tell that his self-reflection pays off. After all, he wouldn't continue pursuing a relationship with a man who outright refuses to wipe his butt because it's "not manly" (yes, that was a real Listener Letter).

Get A Hustle

- He often talks about before *The Read*, he worked long hours at his day job and pursued the things he loved at night. Look where he is now.
- Find your hustle, even if you can't do it full time now. Start small.

Get Some Prayer

- Kid Fury is very religious and connected to God. Even though I myself ran from the church kicking and screaming, I can really appreciate his belief system and apply it to myself. I'd like to think the universe is always looking out for you. Take the time to reflect and meditate, and, most importantly, be good to others.

CHAPTER FOUR

---

1 REASON TO WATCH 13 REASONS WHY SEASON 2

T W: *This article discusses sexual assault and rape that happens in 13 Reasons Why, Season 2. And while I am about to rip a rapist to shreds, I am sensitive to you protecting your mental health. Proceed with caution. Also, if you or someone you know is a rape victim, here is a list of resources that may be able to provide support. Take care of yourselves, we care about you.*

I hear ya, this season of *13 Reasons Why* isn't without issues, and that's putting it lightly. After that overly gratuitous and unnecessary rape scene, I have more than thirteen reasons to throw this series in the trash.

However, let's dig it out of the trash for a second. Wash off the sticky goo and banana peels and focus on the one thing these writers did right.

They told us why Bryce was easily able to commit such heinous acts against women.

It was NOT because he:

- Was abused as a child.
- Was raped himself.

- Was tired of being rejected by women.
- Was acting out any form of trauma and, therefore, was able to get sympathy from viewers.

Bryce was an asshole rapist simply because *he was an asshole rapist*.

That's it.

He had no excuse. He was a privileged, athletic white boy who got anything he wanted. Even in his speech to his mother, he shrugs while admitting, "I wanted her, so I f*cked her."

This is regarding his rape of Hannah Baker. Often in media, we are made to sympathize with a person who has no regard for their victim's feelings. We try to understand their story. It's frustrating to watch and it's just another way of making their victims (and any victims watching) feel powerless.

But not this time. We went into this whole trial knowing that Hannah, Jessica, and even Bryce's girlfriend Chloe, were all, without question, raped by this fucking rich asshole. And it's very clear that this asshole was not sorry.

While it's disheartening to see the jury ultimately believe his fake-ass nerd defense (they decided to give him glasses and make him look "nerdier" so he looks more innocent when he testifies), maybe this will cause viewers of the show to think before they dismiss a victim's statement.

Your rapist can be rich, can be smart, can have anyone they want, can even have a partner that they have consensual sex with, and STILL be a rapist.

I really hope that this begins to change others perception of "The Perfect Victim" and stop making excuses for people who believe that they are entitled to other people's bodies.

CHAPTER FIVE

ROSEANNE, IF YOU DON'T SIT YOUR NOSEY @$$ DOWN SOMEWHERE

B efore we dive in, this post requires a lot of backstory. Think of this as one of those flashback episodes of a '90s sitcom where they have to catch everyone up at the beginning of a two-part episode.

announcer voice Previously on Roseanne…

So Hollywood has decided that nostalgia was an easy moneymaker. The scripts were practically already written, the cast was already there, and some of the set pieces were probably in storage somewhere. Thus, the idea to reboot *Roseanne* was born. The series premiered in the fall of 2018. This was decidedly very different from the original *Roseanne* as it just seemed to fulfill Roseanne's… I don't even want to say political agenda, that seems too nice. They just kind of straight up turn into mean, grouchy, older people. On May 29th, we received further evidence to Roseanne Barr's "ain't shitness" when she tweeted "Muslim brotherhood and Planet of the Apes had a baby=VJ." VJ being in reference to Valerie Jarrett, Barack Obama's former advisor. She wins the award for *Best Way To Avoid Just Giving A Simple Apology* by saying she wrote the tweet because she had taken Ambien, a known sleep drug. Luckily, no one bought this excuse, and since the reboot of *Roseanne* wasn't doing very well anyway, Roseanne would no longer appear on the show. All of this happened within the timing of me writing this article.

And now you're all caught up!

Okay, the *Roseanne* reboot needs a timeout. Even if I have to drag it to the corner kicking and screaming, I've got to just stick to my guns and remain firm. Do not come out until you have learned your lesson.

In the previous episode of this first season of this atrocious reboot, Roseanne's mom does the whole "I'm going to pretend to kill myself to manipulate you into doing what I want" thing (which, if you have ever grown up with a toxic mother that manipulated you in this way, fair warning: it's cringe-worthy to watch). Dan is doing everything he can to ensure that Darlene's son will need therapy in his push to make him more masculine. *Seriously, Dan?* That birdhouse had some amazing craftsmanship in it. Who cares if it's "feminine" (birdhouses are pretty gender neutral if you ask me), let the boy live!

So, in Episode 7, it starts off with Roseanne spying on her Muslim neighbors through some holes in a rake. Obvious spying aside, I'm gonna just go ahead and tell you everything that's wrong with this episode.

"Aww, Roseanne, your Islamophobia is so cute."

Spoiler alert: it's not.

There were many times when Roseanne's racist comments were followed by a laugh track. On top of that, the writers decided to add a side story of Dan being pissed off about a guy hiring "illegals" to do cheaper work.

I don't believe that the current reboot aligns with the original *Roseanne's* line of thinking. Personally, I always thought as much as they looked the stereotypical blue-collar family, they knew what it was like to be different and didn't pull racist bullshit like that. I can definitely tell you there weren't any purposeful hurtful comments toward Muslim neighbors for sure.

What I did not like is that they didn't even truly address her behavior as being wrong or give her any consequences about it. More laugh tracks played the deeper she suspected her new neighbors of being terrorists.

It shows us why "I'm not racist, I have a black friend/family member/co-worker" does not work

Roseanne has a whole black granddaughter who lives with her and still can't see why assuming her neighbors are terrorists is more than a little messed up? What would have happened if she called the police on them? What if that was YOUR granddaughter sleeping in a bulletproof vest every night? But, no, "that's different"? Give me a break

The Brown People Know What They're Talking About, But Their Story Gets Overlooked

There was a Skype call to Mary's mom. Mary is Roseanne's token black granddaughter, and Mary's mom is a soldier who is stationed in Iraq. Roseanne tells her about the neighbors and asks her how can she tell the difference between the good guys and the bad guys. She laughs and tells Roseanne that she has more reason to be afraid of walking around Lanford, where Roseanne and the entire family resides.

Shit, straight up truth. When black folks are getting murdered for something as simple as knocking on a door asking for directions, it's scary as hell out here. But, of course, this line goes straight over Roseanne's head.

When Roseanne learns her neighbors are from Yemen, she says to them, "Oh that country's not even on the travel ban list," to which the Muslim wife answers "Yes, it is."

Again, while this line points out Roseanne's ignorance, it's still put off as cute—as if her behavior towards these neighbors doesn't have the ability to result in some serious consequences. Falsely accusing a Muslim of being a terrorist, especially a family with a small child, is just not okay. There are subtle hints from the family that touches on this, and as a person of color, I picked up on it. But, still, I feel like the seriousness of the situation was played off as a joke.

Here Comes Roseanne to Save The Day, Except Not Really

One of the last scenes takes place in a grocery store, where some asshole who works there decides to make snide comments to the Muslim female neighbor. Roseanne is conveniently standing behind her in line and hears all of this. The cashier adds more insult to injury by asking Roseanne to "carry her groceries to her camel."

It's a sucky, mild occurrence that Roseanne felt safe enough to say something. She tells off the girl, Roseanne-style, that she was rude and was going to bring it up to her manager. She does bring up, in the end, that their family has enough fertilizer to blow up the place. While funny, it doesn't...really tell the girl that her assumptions were wrong.

So, at this point, we are supposed to stand and cheer for Roseanne for standing up to that cashier and to that, I say, "Nah girl, you really didn't do anything."

After this woman leaves the grocery store, her and her family are going to face even more bullshit from the residents from Lanford. Roseanne, her son is terrified to sleep!

That means that the racism they face is way more intense than just a pissy little grocery clerk's comments.

So, congratulations, you did nothing. You must be so proud.

So, Quinzel, what can we do better?

Like I said in the beginning, Roseanne needs a timeout. There needs to be some reflection on if some of her quirks that are shown as "cute" or "funny" are justifying to others who feel the same way that their racist thoughts and actions are also cute and funny. There is no call to action at the end. No "hey, by the way, if you see someone Islamic being harassed, here's what you can do" at the end. Nothing. There is not enough evidence that the writers, ABC, and Roseanne Barr herself, find this behavior appalling.

And to leave you with one last thought, another thing we can do better is to simply ask ourselves, "Do we really need to reboot EVERYTHING?"

CHAPTER SIX

LYRICS THAT HEALED ME: FALL OUT BOY EDITION

I have a confession; I may be stuck in 2005. Yes, back when iPods were a lot bigger, Rhapsody was still a thing, and I spent hours on end listening to a song I didn't know by a band I didn't know on repeat.

That band was Fall Out Boy.

Fast forward to the present and that obsession only grew over time. What still keeps me a Fall Out Boy stan after all these years?

That's right, ladies and gentleman, the lyrics.

I'm a word nerd, which you probably know by now, since I do the writing thing. But something about someone who can just...word. *heart eyes*

Some lyrics just stick with you forever. Let's look at some of the Fall Out Boy lyrics that actually helped me get through some rough times.

"You are what you love, not who loves you"

This lyric was majorly important in a time where I made a decision to distance myself from toxic people for my own mental health. However, toxic people rarely see it this way and use many manipulation tactics to make you feel unlovable. This lyric was my mantra for a good year.

"Put on Your War Paint"

Another long-used mantra of mine. When I was nervous or about to walk into a stressful situation, I could just say, "Quinzel, it's time to put on your war paint," and I was ready to go.

"I Don't Just Want To Be A Footnote in Someone Else's Happiness"

While the song is mainly about an extramarital affair, being a footnote in someone else's happiness can apply to many different situations. This lyric was a wake-up call for me and helped me nope out of a lot of one-sided relationships.

"Before It Gets Better The Darkness Gets Bigger The Person That You'd Take A Bullet For Is Behind The Trigger"

As painful as this lyric is, there's something refreshing when your feelings aren't put into words. When dealing with betrayal of any kind, it can be hard to access your feelings besides hurt and anger. This lyric made me feel less alone.

"May The Bridges That I Burn Light The Way Back Home"

Mmm, yes. Toxic people I have walked away from took

it as my Walk of Shame. Quinzel will be back. Quinzel can't survive on her own. She doesn't wanna burn her bridges with us.

Well, guess what, bitches? I got matches.

"I'm A Stitch Away From Making It And And A Scar Away From Falling Apart"

At times I feel simultaneously okay and not okay. I feel like I'm so close to the finish line, but I cannot take on another boss fight I'm tired and determined. I'm discouraged but riding on faith all at the same time.

And I can feel not okay and everything still feel okay. Ya know?

CHAPTER SEVEN

QUIRK CABIN SNIPPETS

Now we're done with the articles from Quinzel's Quirk Cabin. Just like when reading a magazine, do you ever just need a break from reading articles and need a few listicles to carry you over? Here's some "Top 10" listicles about all things geeky, quirky, and Quinzel-y.

<u>Things No Black Girl Geek Ever Wants To Hear</u>

- "I don't even see you as black" - It's not a compliment to tell someone that you don't see them as who they are.
- "There are no black girls who like comics/anime, etc." - I love it when people adamantly express this all while they are talking to me, a black girl who they know for a fact loves everything in the geeky realm.
- "I want to cosplay as T'Challa from *Black Panther*, should I use the darkest foundation I can find and smear it all over my face" - They

may not say this in these exact words, but it seems that once someone can accept that you are black and a geek, they tend to think the next logical step is to ask you about *blackfacing* as if the answer isn't an obvious and stern "don't."

- "Why are you into 'white people stuff'" - This in and of itself is infuriating because, what do you even mean by this? It's a comment that came out of nowhere, while I am happily enjoying whatever geek indulgence it is this week and the person comes at me to crush me with this.

- "Why can't you like [insert whatever here]?" – much like the above statement, you learn that people enjoy keeping other people in boxes. There's something about a black girl geek that they can't contain and they can't label. They want you in a box that they can contain, but little did they know you are a confetti cannon, designed to erupt and sprinkle little bits of "you" in every direction.

The Progressive Steps That Will Initiate You Into Any Fandom: Quinzel style

- Step 1: Person recommends The Thing: this could be anything from a TV show to a comic book.

- You procrastinate on getting to The Thing: nothing slows me down faster than something that someone recommends to me.

- You completely forget about The Thing: life moves on with your other nerdy interests.
- You suddenly remember The Thing and give it a go: You have maybe an extra five-ten minutes and you think to yourself "meh, why not?"
- You spend the next six to eight months completely consuming The Thing, looking up fan theories, and finding situations where you can insert The Thing into every conversation that you have: Congrats! You have been initiated.

Things I wish I could tell 12-year-old Quinzel

- "Boys Are Exceptionally Stupid" I remember thinking that male approval was it. I was envious of the pretty girls who had all of the guys attention. But honestly, having that affection was not as big of a deal as I made it out to be.
- "You Don't HAVE To Match" Fashion was of the upmost importance in my adolescent years. I don't miss having the feeling that it's so important to dress well and in name brand clothing. But now that I am an adult, I do what I want.
- "You Won't Grow Out Of This" Sure, there are a lot of silly interests I grew out of. But as I've stated, Buffy is just one example of things I would stick with.
- "It Gets Better" I hated this saying back then,

but I can look back with all sincerity and say, it
DOES get better.

Fictional Characters That I've Fallen in Love With

- Augustus Waters from "The Fault in Our
  Stars"- "The Fault In Our Stars" is sort of a
  cult classic, but, as a writer, I love w o r d s. And
  while the character is very sweet and endearing,
  the way he would word things to Hazel Grace is
  very smooth.
- Angel from *Buffy The Vampire Slayer* - As a pre-
  teen, a sweet, tortured soul that could be fixed
  up was my thing. But Angel was a different
  breed. When I was older, I'd love to appreciate
  the punny nature of Angelus. But at the time, I
  just wanted my sweet Angel back. I remember
  watching Buffy and Angel break up in the
  season finale called "Graduation Day" and
  watching him walk away just hurt my entire
  pre-teen heart.
- Stiles Stilinski from *Teen Wolf* - He's cute, he's
  awkward, he's hilariously sarcastic. He should
  have been mine XD.

Video Games That I Have Hilariously Rage Quit

- Sesame Street 123: Astro Grover- I rage quit
  before I even knew what that term was. As a
  very small Quinzel, I remember the level

"Ernie's Magic Shapes" where you had to match two of the same shapes together. It's funny to look back on now, but I remember getting so frustrated that if you accidentally passed up the shape you wanted to match, you had to start all over. I'd turn off that console so quick, it wasn't even funny.

- Paperboy on NES - Why is death trying to attack me? I just want to deliver papers. Gosh!

- Lion King on Sega Genesis - I would find out years later that this game was designed to be hard. Oh not just hard for kids, I mean straight up HARD. When I was younger, I could only play this game at a friend's house on their console, so I had limited time to figure it out which made it even more frustrating. My not so favorite level was trying to jump off all of the animals while "I Just Can't Wait to be King" plays in the background. Not making it through in time was super disappointing.

- Aladdin on Sega Genesis - Same issue as with The Lion King Sega Genesis game. This ish is hard, and it is hard from the beginning. I hate that I can't get very far in this game. But back in the '90s the graphics were amazing.

- The Simpsons: Bart Simpson vs the Space Mutants on NES: This game was another game I was super excited to play, but when Bart would end up hitting something and saying "Eat my shorts" and you had to start all the way over, I would be beyond frustrated and quit so easily.

COMIC CONS AND PROS: HOW CONVENTIONS RUINED MY LIFE

CHAPTER EIGHT

FALLING IN LOVE WITH COMIC BOOK CONVENTIONS

Do you want to know a secret? I didn't attend my first comic book convention until I was twenty-eight years old. For hardcore fans and followers of nerd culture, this may come as a shock. But I wasn't able to find anyone to embrace my nerdiness with, let alone, another black person. Most of my childhood was spent with adults saying that simply, "Black people don't DO that type of stuff."

So, as I've mentioned before, I watched *Buffy the Vampire Slayer* in secret. I also flipped through comic books in the library, but never checked them out. *I was weird enough,* I thought to myself back then, no way I'd draw more attention to myself.

You do hit a point in life, sometime around college, that you realize that people's words are just...words. Those words still most certainly hurt, but it was something about seeing a black girl walk around campus in full goth makeup that invoked a change in me. Suddenly, it clicked. And I dove deeply into geek culture.

Once I was back home from college, I wasn't immersed in the nerd happenings around town, including the local comic con. It wasn't because I didn't want to go, it was because I didn't even know it existed. I stayed in my shell of reading online fanfiction stories, repeating different Buffy predictions and series in my head, and, on occasion, playing a round of Silent Hill, which my mother bought because it was in the clearance bin. Obviously, she paid no attention to the content.

My husband, then boyfriend, took me to my first convention. He actually asked me about conventions on our first date, and I looked at him, puzzled. I had no idea a thing like that existed. But when the realization hit me, it was like he told me he was taking me to Disneyworld. A geeky, magical world awaited me. When I entered my very first comic book convention, I saw something that almost brought me to tears. A fully built, beautiful, blue TARDIS. The sounds that came from my mouth weren't human. I ran, probably faster than if I was being chased, to this gorgeous and glorious construction.

Did I mention I'm a Doctor Who fan? The 10th doctor is my favorite!

For you Doctor Who fans reading this, it was obviously not bigger on the inside, but the manifestation of something I love so much made me unbelievably happy.

Fun Fact: my husband (then boyfriend) would remember this moment of me gushing over the TARDIS. A year later, he would propose to me at our local comic con in front of this same TARDIS.

My first comic con, I was amazed. I was extremely tired at the end of the day. But more importantly, it unlocked a new level of myself where I felt like not only could I be who I was, but there are thousands of people out there just like me.

Conventions ruined my life, yes. They ruined the way I was living before, and I could no longer go back.

There was a freedom to me being able to fully be who I was, and that day, I fell in love.

I fell in love with comic book conventions.

Ok, I know that saying "conventions ruined my life" was misleading, but there is a true con to comic cons. The main one? MONEY! You are either mad that you don't have enough or that you have spent way too much.

Two bits of con advice I can give you: 1) Make a budget and, 2) stick to it.

But I had a new, expensive addiction. I wanted to know more. Getting involved in *Geeky Girl's Guide to Life* gave cons a new life for me. I love talking to all of the vendors. As a member of the press, I wasn't just pitching to sell the idea of my blog for them, I got to know more about them, what they do, and why they do it. A really fun article I wrote was "Cosplay on The Cheap: Naka Kon Panel with FullElven Cosplay." I attended the Cosplay on the Cheap panel and it was extremely informative and fun. I loved learning more about cosplay and cosplay creation.

Speaking of cosplay, one of the most amazing things about being at cons is to meet cosplayers. For those of you who are new to the nerd community, these are the folks who dress up as different characters. Cosplay is a combination of the words "costume" and "play." Most of these people make their own costumes, but some have a seamstress who is amazing and can work from pictures. Either way, it's a fun thing to talk to them and learn more of what they do.

I don't have a great hand at sewing, but I know enough to be dangerous. I majored in Theater and I'm pretty sure they wouldn't let you leave unless you knew how to sew on a button. I can also hem the bottom of my pants because I am excessively short (don't ask, just know my height is short).

That being said, my own cosplays are simple. I've done Lilo from *Lilo and Stich* with a dress and a long straight wig that I bought. And my most favorite cosplay was being a Cards Against Humanity white card that said 'A Sassy Black Woman.'

Simple cosplays, but honestly, I'd say they are the highlight of my cosplay career, but more on that later.

I applied for press at one of my local conventions but was sadly denied. I wouldn't be surprised if you haven't heard of *Geeky Girl's Guide to Life* before reading this book. We are pretty small. But regardless of size, Leslie (owner of the blog) saw something in me and basically gave me permission to go nuts, so I did. And usually at conventions.

So, the blog didn't get me into one big convention, so I attended an anime convention. Now, I am not by the stretch of any imagination, well versed in anime. Of all the nerdy things, it isn't something I had gotten into. But I had always appreciated it, and who was I to knock anime? You're talking to someone who has been a Buffy fan since she was twelve. Fandom and Obsession are my middle name.

Naka Kon was such an amazing experience from the press side. Really taking a step back to observe and see everything that was going on. The panels were amazing, the cosplay was breathtaking, and, at a misfortune to me, the vendor hall graciously took all of my money.

So, I knew then that to continue to experience more cons, I would have to travel further. I learned that there were so many conventions all over the nation. We all know about the famous San Diego Comic Con that packs in tons of people each year, but there's also places like Geek Girl Con, New York Comic Con, and a small, but special, comic con in Chicago known as WakandaCon.

Let's back up a bit and add this to my fandom list if you didn't already know: *Black Panther*.

In the throes of Post-Partum Depression, I wasn't as excited as I initially was about the new Marvel film *Black Panther*. I knew I wasn't going to the theater opening night. I had a two-month-old premature baby and nothing sounded exciting to me.

A friend of mine, who was not a nerd nor into *Black Panther*, immediately noticed something was wrong. The movie was out for a couple weeks already. She asked if I had seen my movie yet. I shrugged. She said, "I'll watch the baby, here's an AMC Gift Card. Also, here's a restaurant gift card so you and the hubs can grab something to eat after. GO!"

I was immediately grateful and also racked with guilt. But going was the best decision ever. I fell in love with *Black Panther* and the world of Wakanda.

So you can imagine how happy I was when I saw the announcement of WakandaCon. A three-day convention of not just *Black Panther* but NERDY BLACK PEOPLE. The people I was always told don't exist. The weirdos just like me.

I wanted to shout at the top of the rooftops how much I loved this con.

I nervously wrote an email for a press request and waited to hear back from Lisa Beasley. Lisa is one of the co-founders of the con. I knew that with a new baby, I wouldn't be able to come up with the funds or the plans to travel, so we came up with a plan for me to cover the event from home that year. This consisted of me using my expertise of Twitter stalking, interacting with folks who attended the panels and events on the day of. Beforehand, I ended up making blog posts of the upcoming events and hyping everyone up as the date was coming up. Afterwards, there were lots of people still posting about their experience, still posting pictures and whatnot, so I did my part to make sure that WakandaCon got as much online visibility as possible.

Lisa Beasley also took a chance on me, just like Leslie. It was like they already knew I had it in me.

Lisa, if you're reading this, I am forever grateful. You took a chance on a sleep-deprived new mom, and I am so happy you let me write for you.

I blogged from home the first year, but I had a full 365 days to plan my travel to Chicago.

With WakandaCon dates announced and my sitter set up while hubby was at work, I set up my plans to get to Chicago.

But you know that saying, "You plan, God laughs."

The weekend of the 2nd annual WakandaCon was somehow exponentially costly for travel. Plane tickets and train tickets were super-duper high. So in the interest of finances, I took the Greyhound Bus.

Taking the Greyhound Bus was such a mistake it wasn't even funny.

It might be the bus ride that goes down in history, but it was a common occurrence of there's.

Pro tip: Don't take Greyhound. Just don't.

In a nutshell, the bus was late, the bus driver cussed at us and almost ran us off the road, we missed the next bus, that bus was four hours late, the security guard in the building yelling at us and telling us we weren't allowed to sit after standing for four hours. The next bus was late. The bus going home was late.

Oh, and on the way home, when I was so close to this ordeal being over, the bus died. The bus DIED, in the middle of the freaking highway.

The road to WakandaCon was hell, but the actual con was the complete opposite.

Entering and seeing everyone's smiling faces was a dream. I, coming straight from an eighteen-hour bus ordeal, missed all but thirty minutes of Friday. My dreadlocks stuck straight up out of my ponytail, frizzy and smelling like potato chips. I'm surprised the registration desk even believed I was Quinzel.

But walking around was like going to my first comic con, expect everyone looked like me.

I met an amazing girl who dressed as Mrs. Frizzle from the *Magic School Bus*. It was a dream I didn't realize that I had, to see a brown skinned science teacher that I adored, right in front of my eyes.

It was a world where I belonged. Where no one accused me of "talking white" or thought that calling my skin color "chocolate" was a compliment that I was just dying to hear (Ew!). Growing up, I never felt I was black enough. But now I was walking next to and sitting in panels with tons of people just like me.

The saddest part of WakandaCon (cause we not even going to mention the effect this had on my wallet. Goodies, everywhere!) was leaving. Everyone I came in contact with realized that WakandaCon was this bubble, and inside it came all of these positive things that nothing negative could penetrate.

But on the good side, it reaffirmed one thing. WE are out here. Our nerdy, scientific, super smart, crying when your favorite characters die, black nerds. Y'all are so lovely.

WakandaCon, along with any other cons, hold a special place in my heart. Let's take a deeper dive into how I spent my time at WakandaCon. And stay tuned because I might sneak another convention or two in there to talk about.

CHAPTER NINE

THE WOMEN BEHIND WAKANDACON ARE TOTAL BAD ASSES

As part of our *Geeky Girls Guide to WakandaCon* series, wouldn't you want to learn about the women behind the con? 'Cause let's face it. Con after con after con after con, female leadership can be, well, almost non-existent. But that's not the case with this convention.

WakandaCon, taking place August 3rd through the 5th in windy Chicago is headed by women who are almost as fierce as the Dora Milaje in *Black Panther*. But even more than that, they are inspiring. Don't think you can reach your dreams? Think you can't win in a game that's stacked against Black women? The road is hard and not without scars, but these three women have proved that you can battle your way to the top.

Wayment, ALL Y'ALL WORK IN THE ARTS??

Yes! Just before I was about to take that Theater degree and toss it in a fire, I learned that Ali Barthwell (Co-founder, Social Outreach), Lisa Beasley (Producer and

Media Relations), and Taylor Witten (Producer and Content Strategist) all graduated from college with arts degrees. Ali attended Wellesley College, Lisa attended LeMoyne-Owen College and Taylor went to Dartmouth College. All three women combined have experience in acting, production, writing, directing, and teaching well after college.

This is inspiring because, as an arts major myself, it's just so validating to see women, black women in particular, out here doing the damn thing.

The Path to WakandaCon is Paved With Friendship

Each of them came to WakandaCon in their own way. "WakandaCon is founded on principles that I feel are personally important to move our people and culture forward." Taylor says about the convention, "Blackness is a spectrum. Out with the old, and limited question of *'are you Black enough?'*" We aim to shift what it means to be Black, culturally, personally, professionally, and expressively. No matter where you land on the spectrum - your journey and experiences shape the culture. We want this to be a movement. We want to create more seats at the table, establish safe spaces for creatives of color, and amplify their voices. *By joining the WakandaCon team, I felt like I had found my tribe.*

Lisa didn't take much convincing to hop on the project, "My friend Ali Barthwell reached out to me and told me that her brother had an idea named "WakandaCon." I really didn't need any further explanation. I knew exactly what it was and exactly why she was telling me he had the idea. Honestly, it didn't take much. I was on board when she said, "Hey, my brother has an idea." I love helping my friends work out their ideas.

"My brothers and I were going to see *Black Panther* a lot and my older brother, David, came up with the name first: WakandaCon," Ali says, while I wonder if she beat me in the number of times she saw *Black Panther*. "He tried to pass it off to Matt and me to organize but we convinced David to lead us. As we started to build this idea, we realized that we needed more help so I recruited Taylor and Lisa who are friends of mine with experience in the areas we were missing. We've been creating and building this thing since that moment. There has been a lot of educating ourselves and learning from other cons and their successes and mistakes."

So...WYD Outside of WakandaCon?

Thing is, each of these women are out here living life, breaking glass ceilings, hell, breaking glass universes. Doors are opening for them all over the place.

Taylor thought she was slipping me a shameless plug, but I was gonna put her on blast anyway. She's got a film project in the works, called *The One I Love*. It's about a Christian couple who face trials and tribulations as they grow in their relationship and faith. Since Taylor is herself a woman of faith, her production of this Indie film comes straight from the heart.

Lisa is, to put it simply, changing the world. She is the co-founder of The Nova Collective which is a company that works to transform corporate culture. I wanted to know if there had possibly been an uptick in a need for this after...how do I put this lightly...? The shitstorm after the election. "The entire diversity and inclusion industry has increased due to the friction caused by the last election. Conversations are happening in the workplace whether people want them to or not and we help companies strategize how to have those conversations. The last election has put a magnifying glass on problems that have already existed in the workforce so I think a lot of the workforce is relieved people are finally talking about it."

I asked each of them "What's the best thing about being a black woman? what's the worst thing?"

Ali hits me with a simple, but truthful, statement. "The most challenging thing about being a Black woman is being a Black woman today and the best thing about being a Black woman is being a Black woman."

"Sometimes I can't tell if people are not listening to me because what I'm saying is actually trash or because they are not used to listening to black women." Lisa tells me "I've often worked in environments where what I say is dismissed because of my identity, but I've learned that is also my superpower. Now I work in groups that value my expertise and experiences. The best thing about being a black woman. Oh geez. I love how I can bend and manipulate my hair in many different ways. I love the skin I'm in. I love being a black woman."

And lastly, Taylor is taking me to church with her answer. "The BEST part about being a Black woman," she says, "is that there is no limit to the type of woman I can be. Black women grace almost every part of the earth. We're literally everywhere, doing all kinds of great things. It's truly inspiring. The challenge is that most people don't see us that way. I often come across people who have such a narrow view of who I should be and how I should act because I am a Black woman. My hope is that WakandaCon exposes us all to a new way of thinking about Black women and provides a better representation of our whole selves."

. . .

Lisa Stole My Dream Job, Y'all

Not really, no. She didn't steal it from me. But I was super jelly to learn that *Lisa Beasley is a friggin' writer for Cards Against Humanity!!*

"Super cool, right?" she says to my green-with-envy self. "I've had the pleasure of working with a lot of the comedians and writers in the room. The head writers thought that I would be a good fit for the room. Because of my other projects taking off, I now work with them as a Remote Contributor."

If You Don't Read Any Other Part of the Article, Read This

All three of these women have been out there making it happen for themselves. So I had to ask them one burning question:

HOW???!!!???

How did you get to where you are today? How can someone like me succeed in this world? How? How? How!

Thing is, not only is Lisa working in the Arts, she is also making changes in Corporate America and has a lot of advice to give. "Big changes start with yourself. In attempting to save myself economically, I've been able to open doors for other people. The experiences that I've had as a black woman in certain industries led me to explore different career paths that could build spaces for people to do the work that they love to do. Selfishly, I wanted a place to work and found that a lot of my friends were having a hard time finding work because most jobs are just trying to fill a diversity quota and would only allow one of us at a time. So instead of waiting for someone to hire me, I created jobs for myself. If you're a black woman and you want to make big changes, think about the why and hold that in your mind often. Knowing why you are doing what you are doing will get you through the tough times. Also, take care of yourself. We are so used to taking care of others that taking care of ourselves seems selfish."

Moving right along to Ali, who gives us the best advice on how to succeed as a black woman. "First, go to therapy," Ali scolds like a Saturday Morning Mama who tells you to get ready to clean all day "or find a restorative hobby." she continues.

"There will be difficult and trying experiences. You won't be able to avoid them completely but remembering that your mental health and security is the most important thing. It's very easy to think that our struggle fuels our creativity or as Black women, we should shoulder the burden and power through but you can't create from an unhealthy place. You need moments to restore you that make you healthier.

I would also say that you are most likely two to three times better than your white counterparts. That's just a fact. And if you're anything like me, you probably work to be perfect before you even try anything because if you fail, there might not be a second chance. That desire to be exceptional only will help you. Don't let that desire to be perfect hold you back from trying something new or become harmful. See why you'll need therapy?

Lastly, rely on your networks. There are more people who are willing to give you advice, guidance, or an introduction than you realize. Asking someone for advice or asking them to tell you their story to success will make them feel important and they'll probably want to help you.

And lastly, Taylor leaves us with advice that will get you through the entire week. Heck, maybe even the year. "I was really hoping to share some deeply impactful life-changing Def Poetry Slam-style advice," she says, "however, this is all that came to mind — Decide. Commit. Succeed. Only you can determine your future and it starts with making a choice."

If these three women can make it, you can too. WakandaCon forever!

CHAPTER TEN

GEEKY GIRLS GUIDE TO WAKANDACON

For my love of all things having to do with Comic Conventions, WakandaCon is a convention that will hold a very special place in my heart. Below are the blog posts where I chronicled my days attending the convention.

WakandaCon Day 1: Throwing Greyhound Under the Bus

I'm not sure if this counts as an official day one, because I didn't get to see the con until about one hour before they closed. You can thank the Greyhound Bus for that one.

This story is one for the podcast, but if you follow my twitter @quinzelee, I gave you a snippet of what happened. From the driver telling us to act like "real" men and women, to driving off the road and telling us to "shut the hell up" when we alerted him of such, to being well over eight hours late to Chicago, this is a story for the ages.

I wish I could say that Greyhound was sorry for this. But being as that Greyhound hasn't done anything but send a copy-*plus*-paste tweet at this point, I have to, for lack of a better pun, throw them under the bus.

You would think that god-awful bus ride would be enough to sour the excitement for my vacation, but no. You could imagine my relief of seeing that purple WakandaCon sign and walking up to the table for my press pass. Everyone had a big smile and was super helpful. If they were at all overwhelmed, I couldn't tell. I did manage to make a quick lap around the vendor hall, so I have a better game plan of where I will be able to stop for Day 2.

I'm super excited to show y'all everything that WakandaCon has to offer. Stay tuned!

WakandaCon Day 2: Cosplay and Cupcakes

Spoiler Alert: *I think WakandaCon may be my favorite con of all time.*

Yeah, I've attended lots of cons. I've volunteered with a few too. But, man, this one is top-notch.

What can I say? The volunteers were great. Seriously, ALL of them. The vendors were extremely friendly. Heck, Leia from *Just Play Entertainment* was nice enough to do a demo of her game Hip Hop Charades with us. It was a hilariously good time.

Family-Friendly and They Mean It

One thing I also loved about the con is that it doesn't just preach about being a family-friendly convention, WakandaCon delivers. They have more than just a play area for kids. Kids have their own panels and even a STEM booth was set up for them. There were no side-eyes at crying children. Overall, the kids seemed extremely happy to be there. I think I'll be bringing my (not so) little Bby-8 next year. I definitely think Leslie should bring her Geeky Baby one year

Panel: Cosplaying While Black

I'm disappointed that I couldn't clone two of me for just that day because there were SO MANY amazing panels and I couldn't go to them all. Some of those panels were "*Melanin and Mental Health,*" "*Taking Black Magic to New Heights: Diversifying the Space Industry,*" and "*Queerkanda.*"

The discussion in the Cosplaying While Black panel revolved around things we already know and experience as black and brown cosplayers. The two biggest takeaways were:

- Black cosplayers get so much more hate than a white person doing the same cosplay.
- Because of that, it can be extremely emotionally taxing to cosplay while black.

We as POC know this, but it was so validating to hear. I hate when I bring up an issue with racism in cosplay and people dismiss me by saying "*Nooooo, we are all the one race: the human race.*"

That's great, but it still doesn't solve the issue of people threatening us and calling us "apes." In 2017, a cosplayer known as Krissy Victory shared a video where she tearfully recounts the hurtful and racist comments targeted at her when she cosplayed as the D.Va from the popular video game, Overwatch.

The panelists shared their pain, but they also shared their strengths. This panel was full of inspirational people who often give back to their communities and are overall strong and positive people. They inspire anyone who wants to cosplay to go out and DO IT. There was even a short slide showing the panelists and their cosplay evolutions. It really proved that your craft gets better over time.

I LOVED all of their cosplays, but my absolute favorite cosplay was Ashhuhlee who was cosplaying as Max dressed as Powerline from *A Goofy Movie*.

For those of y'all who don't know, it's the scene from *A Goofy Movie* where Max tries to woo Roxanne by interrupting an all school assembly and sings "Stand Out" by the fictional (but still legendary) Powerline.

All of these cosplayers worked super hard to put on this panel and it turned out amazing. If you want to get to know them, here are their Instagrams:

Icy Ace Cosplay IG: @d.etheridge.alpha

Outta Line Cosplay IG: @outtalinecosplay

Lusciously_Wicked Cosplay (with Javon Jackson. They are engaged and cosplay together awwww) IG: @Lusciously_Wicked Cosplay

SuperDan6488 Cosplay IG: @danlemon88

Ashhuhlee IG: @ashhuhlee

Suga Bear Co IG: @sugabearco

Cosplay Contest and Parade

Showing again how good this con is to their kiddos, they had the kiddos come out first and I about drowned in cuteness. The *awwwww*s never stopped.

The adults still came and showed out. Congrats to the winner Dr. Esquivel Ph.D. The costume lights up!!!

After the contest. There was a cosplay parade. As the line of cosplayers circled around the convention center, they began Jabari Tribe chants that echoed throughout the halls of the convention center.

I L I V E D!

Convention Cupcakes

I'll admit, whether I'm working or doing press at a con, I am not the greatest at remembering to eat. I know I need to take care of myself, but it is what it is. My mind just isn't on food.

So imagine my surprise as I came across this lovely booth with cupcakes and chocolate turtles. Sweet Tooth Confections by Ariel "Cocoa" Scott was a lifesaver at that moment. But when I tell you how DELICIOUS this cupcake was...*woo chile*... I am so sad I don't live in Chicago. But she did say she would try to see about shipping cupcakes in the future. So that's good. You will hear me shout from the rooftops if that happens.

Overall, it was an amazing day at an amazing con. I am a die-hard fan now. WakandaCon forever. I don't want to leave.

WakandaCon Day 3: Do I Really Have to Go Home?

Do all good things really have to come to an end? Can't we just keep going and going and cue music for "It's So Hard To Say Goodbye."

I woke up this morning feeling two opposite emotions. Super excited to spend one last day at WakandaCon and also super sad that I only had one last day at WakandaCon.

I ran into Lusciously Wicked Cosplay and her fiancé

again (shout out to that amazing SNOWoncye cosplay which was a mashup of Snow White and Beyonce) and we hugged and were so glad to run into each other one last time.

The amazing thing about this con is it's not just a love for all things *Black Panther*, it's a love for all black people. Black people of all ages, genders, sexual orientations, college degrees, ALLL kinds of black people were welcomed here.

That isn't to say (I can't believe I even have to say this) that this con is against white people or ONLY for POC. It's all about the openness of the atmosphere. It's about how comfortable I was to just exist.

I wasn't a black blogger. I wasn't a black fan. At WakandaCon, I was simply Quinzel.

Panel: Writing While Black

Now listen, y'all already know that I am a writer. So this panel was exclusively for me and for my needs XD. But let me share with you a couple of really cool quotes I heard from the panelists:

- "You can't revise a blank page."
- "No one can write that story the way that you do."

I can't say enough good things about this panel!

Panel: Closing Ceremonies with The Founders

As much as I want to beg for more time, this was the final panel that marked the end of the con.

The founders of WakandaCon thanked everyone and

gave the floor to anyone who wanted to say anything. What followed was an outpouring of thank yous that was enough to bring the founders and everyone in the room to tears.

Also, a couple got engaged during the closing ceremony. Y'all know I'm a sucker for romance.

Like I mentioned in Day 2, if I have one regret with this con, it's that I can't do everything. Some things that I missed out on that I regret now are:

- Shuri's Room: The Official WakandaCon Code-a-Thon: Seriously bummed because I've always wanted to know how to code. Everyone who stopped in, whether they already knew how to code or not, loved it.
- Gaming Marathons: I had hoped that since it was going down all weekend that I could catch a sneak in the gaming room but I did not. I know there was a Mortal Kombat and a Smash Bros. gaming competition and I would have been down to watch (and maybe play) that.
- Queerkanda: That was a panel I would have especially loved to see for myself. But it definitely got OUTSTANDING reviews. Next year, Quinzel, next year.

This was a hard, hard con to leave. Usually, the Con Depression sets in after I've had some time to reflect. But this...it just sucks because I don't want to go back to real life. I want to code and I want to see people walk around in amazing costumes and I want to be comfortable at the intersection where my blackness and nerdiness meet and...

Con depression can really make you spiral. But it's important to know that WakandaCon isn't just one weekend. It took all of these wonderful people to plan this, to attend this, to vend wonderful merchandise at this, and to network and speak about this.

We out here, WakandaCon just gave us a way to all be in the same space at the same time.

I still don't wanna go, though #crying. Luckily, there are other conventions aside from WakandaCon. As much as WakandaCon will always hold a special place in my heart, there is something special and magical that I can find in each convention that I have attended. Let's take a look at walk down comic convention lane.

CHAPTER ELEVEN

QUINZEL'S COMIC CONVENTION SNIPPETS

C lose your eyes. I want you to imagine that you are in a building with 10,000 geeks. Some are dressed up. Some are wearing funny t-shirts. The building smells like hot dogs, cardboard signs, and pure excitement (if that has a smell). Now open your eyes. Read below for my comic convention snippets!

Dream Conventions to Attend

- SDCC aka San Diego Comic Con - The CON! I have been to San Diego Convention Center during TwitchCon, and while that convention was packed, I am sure that SDCC is even more packed!
- Geek Girl Con - I mean, I write for Geeky Girls Guide to Life so... I feel like this is definitely somewhere I would fit in at! Located in Seattle, Washington, this con celebrates women in

science, technology, comics, literature, gaming, and so much more! I'd love to attend.

- WonderCon - Any convention that is in the same city as Disneyland is bound to get my vote! They have had amazing celebrities attend over the years and their panels are epic. One of these days I will be able to go!
- BlerdCon - a combination of the words "black" and "nerd," BlerdCon just sounds like somewhere I need to be. This con has gone on for a few years now, so I am excited to watch it grow even more!

Best Celebs I've Met at a con

- Darryl McDaniels (DMC of Run DMC) - When I attended Planet ComicCon, I had no idea that he published his own comics through his publishing house *Darryl Makes Comics*. He was really friendly and I loved learning about his geeky side.
- Stan Lee - That convention where I got proposed to at? Well, we immediately went over to take our picture with Stan Lee. I remember feeling like he was so tired, but still so happy to meet his fans.
- Karen Ashley/Walter Jones/David J. Fielding - My husband is a HUGE Power Rangers fan. We volunteered at a local, smaller convention and was able to assist in Celebrity Row. Karen Ashley and Walter Jones were the most enthusiastic and friendly people you could ever

meet. Their positivity was absolutely contagious. I got to talk to David J. Fielding for a bit and learn about his book. We talked about our love for writing. Honestly, I probably wouldn't have had the nerve to write this book without his encouragement.

- Felicia Day - I saw her for maybe five seconds, but it was amazing.

Convention Survival Kit

- Cash: As the saying goes, cash is king. If ATMs are down and credit card machines aren't sure if they're swiping or tapping, cash will save you in these situations.
- Tissue: This is something I often forget and always end up with a situation where I need one. Just grab a small pack of travel tissues and you'll be at the ready if you have a runny nose or if you're crying your eyes out over meeting David Tennant.
- Refillable water bottle: Not soda, not juice, straight up H2O. And don't just think you're going to be there for eight to twelve hours and only drink one small water bottle. Most convention centers have water fountains, so you aren't subjected to buying water. Just bring you a nice, insulated water bottle so you can stay hydrated all day.
- OTC Pain Relievers: Just in case to get you through the day. Sure, you may not need them, but you'll be glad you had them if you do.

- Comfy Shoes: Or have a change of comfy shoes for the end of the day so you aren't limping back to your car when the con is over.
- Step Tracker: It's not required, and most people have a step tracker they can download on their phone. I just think it's fun to see how many steps you take in a weekend. Spoiler alert: it's going to be a lot.

Conventions are nice, but behind every person you pass in that vendor hall, every cool cosplay, and every panelist, is a parent, a sibling, maybe even a grandparent. All of us are connected to some kind of family unit. Some of them are great! And some of them…well, I'll let you read on.

FAMILY: AN F-BOMB TO AN F-WORD

CHAPTER TWELVE

"FAMILY WAS ALWAYS AN F-WORD TO ME." -
DEADPOOL

Content Warning: Description of toxic and abusive families. Proceed with caution.

I laughed a little too hard at that quote in *Deadpool 2* (did I mention that I love movies? More on that later). My laugh echoed through the auditorium for a second too long.

It wasn't just the gritty, breaking the fourth wall humor that had me cackling just a little too hard at that moment. Without spoiling too much, Wade Wilson reveals to his girlfriend his biological family woes, which brings him to saying this quote that gave me a chuckle. I laughed because, for me, family was always my F-word. Or, really, my f-bomb. And at any moment, it could explode.

There were good moments in my family of origin, don't get me wrong. Things like getting my first dollhouse on Christmas Morning, the smell of honey baked ham for Easter Dinner, even the sound of my mom's keys jingling down the school hallway because I knew she was picking me up early to go to McDonald's.

But like any other bomb, when this bomb goes off, it

destroys everything in its path. It doesn't care what all you have worked for or what good moments you have been maintaining until now. Eventually, it all just blows up.

I talk about my family on the blog at times. You see mentions of Hubby and my adorable little Bby-8 (who I charmingly nicknamed after the Star Wars droid, Bb-8) and that's the happier, brighter sight of my family.

But my F-Bomb origins, where I came from, I discuss that on the blog from time to time because it explains a lot of who I am and how I got to where I am today. Whether it is making a post on a holiday that it's okay if you don't spend the day with family or letting people know it's okay to message the page for the day, I make it known that I come from imperfect circumstances. And try to pave the way for people like me, to not only find their chosen family, but find family in yourself.

When I told you earlier that I was often known as a "white girl," even though it mostly came from kids in my school, this particular version of teasing actually originated in my home. I was always nerdy, for as long as I could remember. In fact, I was also always a writer for as long as I could remember too. I think that was a moment of contention between me and the rest of my family. "You always so…different" I would often hear, hissing through gritted teeth. It would take me a while to understand that this had nothing to do with me and everything to do with them.

There were smaller things that happened, like the teasing, and there was also just outright emotional, mental, and at times physical abuse. With all of these things being witnessed (as they often are in black families) one thing people felt the need to constantly remind me of is that my mom was only doing her best. But the truth is, she was doing what was easy for her. While she wasn't as outright evil as some of my family members and certainly not as physically abusive, she checked out emotionally. I understand now it was to ease some of her own trauma, but it came with the cost of our relationship. One thing she outright refused to do, not until I was much older, and she needed something, was to say the words "Quinzel, I love you."

I talk about my mom but I have to have a father somewhere, right? My father…it feels weird to say "my father." If you pay attention, you know that I never mention having a dad. Because I don't actually know the man. I honestly don't.

He exists. My parents were even married—if you can believe that. But court records show they divorced when I was one year old.

My mom would never explain to me why, or who he was or speak his name. I remember being six years old, after finding out from my classmates that they all had dads and demanding to know where mine was. I had a great answer for them. "Oh, I don't have one" I'd say with a smile. I'd close my eyes and just imagine my baby-self being formed out of thin air, a nurse wheeling my mother to her car, ready to take me home.

"You have to have a dad, stupid," the girls on the playground told me. "Everyone has one. Where is he?" At that moment, whether they noticed or not, my face fell. I began searching blank spots in my brain. *Where was he?*

"Isn't there a man who's around or visits you sometimes? It's probably him."

One thing you need to know about my mom. Although she wasn't affectionate to us, she loved men. Not a lot of men. She prided herself about not "parading a bunch of men" around her young girls. But the few that she met, she fell hard for. There were men she pecked on the cheek or whispered in the kitchen that she loved them, but I couldn't even get a hug from her after school because she was too tired.

My older sister had a dad who she would go visit in the summertime. But I do remember crying at the door wanting to go too and mom yelling "no, she is going with her dad."

Her dad, she would say, meaning not *my* dad.

After that conversation with the kids, I went home to excitedly ask my mom who my dad was. I took my back-pack off and asked her "Mom, where is my dad"

The TV was blaring and she stared ahead of me, blinking as if I wasn't there. "Mom, where is my dad?" she kept staring ahead, like I wasn't even there. So I asked again, and again.

Her face was unchanged. She didn't seem mad or sad. Just that she wanted to tune me out.

In my child-like mind, I just assumed that she didn't hear me because of the sound of the TV.

I moved in front of the TV, blocking it with my body.

"Mom, where——" but I wouldn't get the chance to finish that sentence.

"Girl, move!!" she boomed, effectively snapping out of her stoic look.

"Mom——"

"Go to your room NOW."

Back then, this was a punishment, but once I got older, this was a sanctuary, a safe space. She would later grow to resent sending us to our rooms by sarcastically yelling "fine, go to your rooms, RUN!"

I had tried to discuss this with her several more times. I even decided that since she was tuning me out at home, I'd ask her in public. Once, we were at the grocery store, and I was reminded about my dad-less status by a little girl, no older than four, extending her arms out to a man and saying sweetly, "Daddy! Daddy!" While walking in the grocery store, I focused on the two of them.

What does having a dad feel like? I thought to myself as I continued to watch them. The man scooped the little girl up in his arms and my chest began to feel warm. I longed to feel that love.

Holding my chest to mimic a hug, I asked my mother in a loud voice "Where's my dad?!" I could already feel the warm feeling starting to fade away, and I started to fidget my feet with anxiety.

"Be quiet!" she'd said through her teeth. The warning was clear, but confusion, frustration, and now jealousy were swirling around in my head. Why did the little girl get a dad and I didn't? I wanted my mom to tell me why.

I decided to enter dangerous territory and stand my ground firmly. I planted my feet firmly to stop fidgeting and looked her in the eye. I pushed my words and breath out of my belly and let my feelings come to the surface. "Where is my dad? Where is he? Everyone else has a dad and I don't and I—"

She snapped around and grabbed my arm, hard. Looked me in my face until they were almost touching. In a whisper, but almost poisonous tone, she said "Shut up! You hear me? How dare you talk to me like this!" Her breath was hot on my cheek, nails digging deep into my arm. At this point, my instinct was to twist away, say "ow," say anything. But I shut down. I let my arm go limp so she knew I wasn't running away. Even though she was whispering, it felt like the entire store stopped and was staring at the both of us. Except it didn't feel like they disapproved, it felt like we were their entertainment in the moment, like they hoped something would escalate. For a moment, I could tune out part of what she was saying, just enough where I knew when to say "yes" and when to say "no," And just like that, it was over. She was back to perusing groceries like nothing happened. Others in the store went about their shopping. I had thought the issue was resolved until she'd lectured me in the car about how much I embarrassed her in public.

Though it wouldn't make any sense to be embarrassed. There were plenty of people who I knew that were walking around here without a dad. I guess she felt some kind of way about it being addressed. Like if she just raised me long enough and never said a thing, I'd never ask.

I often wonder how often her mother did that to her.

What I had in lieu of a non-existent father was a trio of uncles ranging from absent to downright evil. One in jail, one an example of a terrible father, and another who measured his success with booze, women, and how often he used his fists.

I won't get into the nitty gritty details, but you should know that my earliest memory of one of them was beating my mom in the face and giving her a black eye when I was four. He would often yell loudly about wanting to be respected. But he didn't want respect, he wanted to be feared.

I began my journey with a therapist in my late twenties, in secret to my family, who recommended I go Low Contact. Low Contact is a phrase used to describe a specific way in which you keep in contact but on your own terms. For my own mental health, this was to emphasize the LOW.

I started with an out-of-town road trip my family was going to. I still communicated with my mother and other members, but me and the therapist agreed I attend family functions only if 1) I could leave when I wanted, because 2) I drove myself.

Well, this was far enough that I would be carpooling and if a fight broke out, I couldn't leave. So this event was my first practice in saying no.

Saying no wasn't received well in my family. You don't have a voice, you just listen. You don't push back. Because family is everything.

See, most people have the last part down. They live by the saying "family is everything." The difference with my family of origin is that family is everything because Quinzel keeps her mouth shut.

So I didn't bring it up until my mom asked me. "I'm not going" I told her. While this initially felt very freeing, I was still unlearning the concept that telling your elders "no" is disrespectful. "No" seemed like this word too ominous to even breath in the direction of my family. I had gotten by, skimming the top level of the toxicity, by being agreeable. So any positive feelings were immediately over-shadowed by guilt and bracing myself for an inevitable negative fallout.

Instead of leaving it at her usual "well you're grown and that's your decision," she and I both knew that wasn't going to be the end of it.

Remember when I mentioned the mental abuse? From that point until the day they left for their fourth of July trip, I got various phone calls from various family members. They started out loving and "we would really love you to go" to guilt-tripping "so you don't care about your family anymore" to downright threatening "if you don't go I won't help you with XYZ. Don't ever ask me for anything again. You're such a brat."

But you know what? Spending that holiday alone was the best thing I ever did for myself. I wasn't on edge or watching the door if a fight broke out. I wasn't holding back tears after being called a "white girl" or my lack of dating or just being "different" in general. That night, I cuddled up in bed in my one-bedroom apartment, snuggled in with a bowl of ice cream. And watched fireworks on TV. It was heaven.

I was right to avoid the trip. The Worst Uncle decided to drink, as per usual for him. After feeling hurt that my older sister didn't want to take a picture with him, he began cussing and threatening to beat up not only her, but anyone who came to her defense. Also per usual for him.

He would never apologize. My grandmother would tell us not to make him so angry. Even later, she and my mother would say this event never happened.

At random points in my life, my older sister would tell me my dad was abusive, and that's why I never saw him. This made me wonder if my dad was as bad as my uncles. Sadly, I will never know. I've watched them do unspeakable things and still be welcomed with open arms. So while I can say that there's a chance he could have been, there's a bigger chance that my mom just wanted me, along with my dad, to just disappear.

Then there was *The Night I Didn't Look Back*. The night the F-Bomb exploded.

I had been working with a therapist on establishing boundaries and just saying no.

One thing about my mom is that she is completely computer illiterate, so she often needs help with the computer. There's usually a virus (because other people in the family realized this was the best computer to sneakily access porn) and it usually takes hours to wipe, reset, and reinstall. She called me to come fix this computer. I started to say I could do it this time, but after this she would have to find someone else.

And just like that, the protective shield of being agreeable went out the door.

Something to note that my therapist told me later.
Boundaries aren't to make people respect you more. In
fact, most of the time they will hate you for it. It will not
make your relationship better. It's for you. It's for you to
have a better relationship with yourself.

She used all of her tactics. How I was nothing. How no
one would love me. How I was an ungrateful brat and she
sacrificed everything for me. How no one would love me.
And how I was nothing.

The therapist I was seeing told me the power of "I'm
hanging up right now," so I did. And this, this was the nail
in the coffin for any kind of relationship I was going to
have with my family.

My mom immediately drove to my place, yelling that I
better open the *fucking* door. I didn't realize that on her way,
she called half the family. After I let her in and let her
scream at me, my phone, on silent began ringing. After she
left, I would receive a barrage of messages from my sister,
aunts, and grandmas about how I was disrespectful, and
how they should kick my ass.

That was the night I was done. That was the night I
was breaking this cycle.

I started out by moving and not telling anyone where in
the city I was moving. My lease was up. I honestly didn't
think it would work, that eventually someone would find
out. I kept my number the same but didn't answer it
anymore. Except one fateful day I did, months later. The
phone number was private and I thought it was the
doctor's office. It was an older cousin, calling to say "I just
wanna say fuck you, you blocked me on Facebook and I
didn't even do shit to you."

I kick myself this day for engaging with her as long as
I did. Trying to convince her that I care, but she already
had an agenda. She already knew what happened

between me and my mom. She knew and she agreed with her.

My biggest regret is that I did not tell her that her husband has been having sex with my older sister for the past eight years at that point. That her anger at me was only so she never had to face her cheating, narcissistic husband. The men in my family, while horrible, they had the armor to block taking any kind of responsibility for their shitty actions.

After her conversation, I scream-cried in my car. I was also afraid she would shoot me because, well, she had taken gun classes and had a ball of anger I have never dealt with.

I had nightmares for days that she was coming after me. I rotated in my head every day how she said, "You ain't shit. You'll never be successful."

But after my bout of self-pity, I had some logic. My mom and grandmother are enablers, my older sister is abusive to her kids, I have an abusive alcoholic uncle and an abusive pothead uncle. My cousin was ready to blow at any moment. And my mother had a constant rotation of terrible men in our lives.

Things were never going to change. More bombs were just going to drop.

I texted my mother and let her know what had happened with my cousin. That I was changing my phone number and that I couldn't take it anymore.

Know what? She texted me back. "Okay."

I tried Low Contact for about six months. I wanted time to reflect. Maybe things would change enough for me to feel good enough to come back. But instead, things only escalated and got worse. As long as they could contact me, as long as they could find me, nothing would change.

I was tired of family being an f word. I accepted that I wouldn't have the kind of love that I craved.

Boy, was I wrong.

I kept walking by this damn cell phone store, knowing I needed to get my phone fixed. Day after day I walked by this store until finally, I went in. I smiled and approached a guy. I thought nothing of it. I had promised myself to stay single for a year and, at this point, was even done having Friends with Benefits. I wore this red lacy dress with a sweetheart neckline. His eyes were the kindest I had seen on a man.

We went to a table for him to clear my phone, and he was able to see I had like five Doctor Who Apps and a couple Sonic the Hedgehog apps.

"Do you like Doctor Who?" he asked me.

We go back and forth, nerding out while he is logged in and fixing the phone. Before I leave, he gives me the store card and tells me to call if I have any problems. He also gave me his personal number and told me I can call him anytime to talk about nerd stuff.

I almost took my aunt's horrible advice. NEVER call first, you look desperate. I was always a social person, so I hated this rule, but I had been burned by it before. Looking TOO eager. So, I texted him "Hey, this is Quinzel. It was nice meeting you today." I'd said I'd give him three days, and if he didn't respond I would just delete the number.

He responded that night.

Constant conversation about life, nerdy things, and even heartbreak drew us closer.

And the day he proposed marriage to me, he paid homage to that night we met. He proposed in front of a big blue Doctor Who Tardis.

This man who became my husband was different than

any other family I ever had. He was kind, he never communicated with his fists, but overall, he was always my biggest fan. As I'm typing this, he's probably standing over me telling me to write.

I can honestly say that our wedding was one of the best events of my life. I wore a pretty, white dress, our table centerpieces were board games, and we danced the night away just playing "Just Dance" on Xbox. It was beautiful. It was peaceful, and I couldn't have asked for a better day.

And just when I thought family couldn't get better, we had even more in store.

We found out we were pregnant about two months after the wedding. I was thrilled, but I was also very sick. I spent most of my pregnancy throwing up. Sometimes even unable to keep water down, I would make regular stints to the ER and get an IV to rehydrate.

You know that scene in Twilight: Breaking Dawn? Where Bella is pregnant and she's lost weight and her eyes are sunken in and she looks like hell? That was me, the entire time.

The thing is, I just wanted this little one to survive. I'd cry thinking he wasn't getting enough food because I was throwing up all the time.

He was going to be a part of this family. And I loved him, and I didn't want to fail him.

Fun fact: Beyoncé and I have a lot in common. Not... actual talent or anything, she absolutely wins in the singing/dancing/performing category. But we both had severe preeclampsia, and it is no joke.

My blood pressure was 280 over 100. I told them that was weird, I felt fine. This happened twice at around seven months. They told my husband we needed to check my blood pressure at home. He had me lie on the couch as I protested. I didn't feel any worse than I felt the whole time I was pregnant anyway.

I don't know what the last one read. He just said, "We're going," and off to the hospital we went. After trying to get my blood pressure down for several hours, the nurse told me "You're going to be having a baby very soon."

My response: "But I haven't washed his socks yet!"

While the nurses laughed at my outburst, the truth is that I didn't feel prepared for motherhood. People doubted me because I was too sick, too geeky, too inexperienced with children. How could someone like me with a past like mine raise a healthy, happy child?

During my pregnancy, I read A LOT of books. I learned some good nuggets of knowledge (like, did you know babies under one shouldn't eat honey? 'Cause I didn't before I read that), but mostly—and I can't stress this enough—beginning the journey of healing my childhood trauma helped me.

People warned me that when Bby-8 was born, that I would probably feel nothing. While they reassured me it was okay and there were things I could do to bond with him, I still felt sad about the idea. I was worried I would be just like my mother.

But when I saw him for the first time and they laid him on my chest, I felt such an intense love I've never felt before. Seconds before I asked my husband if he has hair. He laughed and said yes. Bby-8 cried the whole time the doctors were cleaning him, but when they brought him over to me and he could hear my heartbeat through my chest, he was instantly calm. I looked at my husband whose eyes were misty from tears and now wetting his medical face mask.

This. This was worth waiting for. My f-word. My bomb-ass family.

Don't grab the tissues just yet. Okay, you can grab them, but come back here and read some articles all about family.

CHAPTER THIRTEEN

_____

CRYING BEHIND MY SUNGLASSES AT PRIDE: HOW 'FREE MOM HUGS' WAS LIFE-CHANGING FOR ME

I t is now a tradition that my spouse, kiddo, and I attend our local Pride festival each year. It's one of my favorite things to do because Pride is like this little force field of awesome where the daily effects of homophobia and willful ignorance about sexuality cannot penetrate it. However you identify, there is something beautiful about people coming together in one place to be exactly who they are with no judgment or interference from anyone else.

Also, Pride is just a heckin' good time. There's a Ferris wheel. It's the bomb-diggity.

Only in the last few years of my life have I been able to enjoy Pride. I have an aunt (who I'm no longer in contact with for soon-to-be obvious reasons) who would laugh about Pride. She would say horrible things about going to Pride just to "sight-see" (I'm using a better word here) and I was traumatized by this. I was so afraid there were hundreds of straight people like her at Pride who just saw everyone there as "entertainment" (using a different word again as not to trigger).

My first year at Pride made me see that someone with my aunt's mindset would never last a day at Pride.

As accepting, loving, and fun as Pride is, you would think that would be enough to make me cry behind my sunglasses. But no. The first year I attended, I was awestruck. I completely took in the energy around me and felt the positivity, the freedom to *just be*, running through my veins.

I was happy. I was free. But I didn't cry. *Not yet...*

Back to the relevancy of bringing up my aunt earlier, I am not in contact with anyone in my family. They don't know where I live or have my number. And I pray to all of the gods, every last one of them, that I don't run into them.

So I'm living life without my birth family. It's painful, but I have amazing friends. But, as amazing as my friends are, even as amazing as YOU ARE because you're reading this right now and supporting me, I crave the love of a parent, the unconditional love of a family. I love my friends, my spouse, my beautiful baby. I'm more than prepared to catch them when they fall, *but who is there to catch me?*

Back to Pride: it was a sunny Sunday morning. So sunny, in fact, I came armed with a new pair of sunglasses, so I wouldn't, you know, go blind.

As I walked down the vendor hall, I notice a group of women wearing shirts that say *Free Mom Hugs* embracing a group of people. A man also wears a *Free Dad Hugs* shirt and my throat catches.

Just to reiterate as I've talked about this before, I've got my own set of daddy issues. *The Free Dad Hug* was just what I needed. And I wasn't even expecting to get a Dad Hug that day. I never talk about my dad and it's because I've never met him. My parents were married, but they divorced when I was just one year old. He's been gone ever since. The only picture I've seen is of him looking down. I've never even seen his eyes. None of the adults in my life would willingly give me any information about him.

So I've never in my life been hugged by my own dad. And my biological uncles...well, they aren't the hugging type.

The man wearing the *Free Dad Hugs* shirt made eye contact with me and waved. He asked if I would like a hug. I knew I could say no, and I knew my eyes were covered with the sunglasses, thus any visible emotion coming to the surface. But I nodded.

I didn't think this hug would spark tears. That a simple pat on the back would start a chain reaction of tears hitting my sunglasses like hot water from a hose. I pulled away to subtly wipe the tears from under my sunglasses. I cleared my throat and said an audible and quick "thank you."

I will blame it on my upbringing, but I hate hugging men that I don't know. I'm always afraid that a hug is signing a contract with a hidden clause that I don't realize until it's too late. But in that moment, I felt safe and I felt appreciated. Hell, I felt loved.

After I said "thank you," the group noticed my spouse and baby and I introduced them. The entire *Free Mom Hugs* group clamored around little Bby-8 in the stroller, exchanging more heartfelt hugs with me. They hugged my spouse. They told me that my baby was beautiful. They told me they were proud of me as a mother and that I was doing a good job. And then I teared up again. Not hard enough for them to (blatantly) notice, but enough to where the sunglasses fogged up quicker. Thing is, I wasn't sad, *I was relieved.*

Something in that interaction allowed me to unpack

something that was heavy, something that was weighing me down. In that short moment, I felt that all of my hard work to better myself was worth it. I had been so used to being torn down, so used to hearing negative talk from my bloodline that receiving a hug and being told that someone is proud of me was enough to bring me to tears.

Free Mom Hugs didn't just change my life, they helped me heal. They gave me something that I've needed for a long time. If anyone from *Free Mom Hugs* is reading this right now, I want to tell you this: by being a temporary mom and dad to me, you all helped me be a better mom to my son. And I thank you for that with my whole heart.

CHAPTER FOURTEEN

I HAD PPD SO BAD, I DIDN'T EVEN WANT TO SEE BLACK PANTHER

Yeah, girl, it was that bad.

In December I had my first very own geeky baby. I wasn't due until the end of January 2018, but Bby-8 was ready to make his grand entrance.

I won't go into the details of the birth, just imagine I was a first-time mom saying "what?" and "holy fuck" a lot.

But I had some baby bottles purchased, had some onesies and sleepers laid out, and a good stock of diapers. I was prepared.

What I was not prepared for was Postpartum Depression.

On the cusp of the Black Panther premiere, I went from enthusiastically talking about this movie for months to feeling like nothing, not even Black Panther, could give me joy.

When most people think of postpartum depression, they recall some pretty awful news stories that I can't bear to repeat. Even the doctor asks you in a dry tone, "have you had thoughts of harming your child?"

Oh? No. I like the baby. It was me that I didn't like.

Since what I had only known about postpartum was from the media, I didn't think I had it because my feelings weren't towards the baby, they were toward me.

I felt hopeless. I felt inadequate. I cried for four hours a day. I felt like I was the most awful person and couldn't tell you why I thought that but the feeling was strong. I couldn't eat, but I just chalked it up to the nausea.

It wasn't until my husband took notice that I was able to get what I needed.

He kinda got a head start. Bby-8 was a preemie and spent a few weeks in the NICU, so the nurses pulled him aside and gave him some signs to watch out for. He comforted me and he took the time to make sure I ate. When he asked me about buying tickets to Black Panther and I just shrugged, he *knew* something was really wrong.

So why am I telling you this story? Because as Geeky Girls, we know the things we love and give us joy. Mental illness tries to take that away from us. But if we can stay ahead and know when it's coming, we can win this fight.

Still, I wasn't enthused about leaving the house. I really did not want to go.

So, I'm gonna offer a bit of advice for anyone struggling with any type of depression: If you're offered the chance to venture outside and you really don't want to: *go anyway*.

After leaving the movie theater, I not only had to thank my husband for pushing me to go, but my best friend who paid for my movie tickets and babysat just so I could go. And she isn't even a big comic fan, she just knew it was important to me.

I walked out refreshed and ready to face the day. It would still take time to see a large improvement in my PPD (I'm doing much better now) but that small thing really made a huge leap in my recovery.

So again. Leave your house. Do it. Don't abandon the things you love. Those things won't resolve the PPD completely, but damn it helps.

So, I'd like to know if any of you have dealt with depression, postpartum or otherwise. Tell me all about your coping mechanisms, your support people, and your "aha" moments.

If you know someone having issues with postpartum depression, here are some helpful links:

http://www.1800ppdmoms.org/

www.postpartum.net

CHAPTER FIFTEEN

"PM ME IF I'M FRIENDS WITH YOUR ABUSER:" WHY THAT $#%T DOESN'T WORK

T*W: The following article discusses sexual trauma, abuse, and assault from a victim's perspective. While it does not give details, it does go in depth on an emotional level and may be triggering for some. Proceed with caution.*

Chances are if you're reading this, you've been a victim of sexual misconduct, harassment, or assault at some point. Stats can only account for those who come forward. It does not account for those suffering in silence at every Bill Cosby or Harvey Weinstein water cooler talk at the office.

While you can usually plug in your earphones and drown them out while you work (guilty), there is just one Facebook post that I can't seem to get away from.

It's a lovely little picture with a white background. It reads: "If I am friends with your abuser PM me, that will change. I see you. I hear you. I believe you. Your story matters." Ah, a nice little meme. A way for your friends to show solidarity with you. A chance to have someone not only believe you but take action.

So... Why do I not feel great about this pic being shared?

First of All, This Should've Been Done A Long Time Ago

It should not take a meme. It should not take a high profile court case. It should not take several high profile court cases.

Because some of y'all knew. But felt I was too drunk. Felt my "no" wasn't clear enough. Felt it didn't count because we were dating. Felt I was sleeping around anyway.

So don't pretend you're my ally now.

So This Is Awkward, My Abuser is Your Significant Other or Family Member

There's a level of pain seeing someone on your friends list, cuddled up, smiling with your abuser. Your abuser has friends, your abuser gets engaged, your abuser has kids.

But what's even more painful is seeing that mutual friend post something with your abuser. Maybe you don't even realize they are connected until it comes up in your feed. But it remains: do I tell the truth to the mutual friend? Do I risk being called a liar? What is that going to do for my healing?

Sending A Name, Just A Name, No Details, Could Make Me Relive My Trauma

Because that name is ruined for me now. That name is forever printed in my head surrounded by fear, anger, hurt, and confusion (gaslighting is a bitch!).

I can't type that name, because it's at the very top of an

unstable tower and typing that name would be the final structure to have it all come crashing down.

There's so much fear of being called a liar, of you wanting to press for details, and also that I just may never stop crying after typing that name.

I just need you to know. It hurts.

Okay, So What Should We Do Instead?

You need action. A meme is a passive gesture. Anyone can share a meme. But what do you plan to do after you get that name? Are you really going to block them? Are you going to confront them? Cut them out of your life?

You gotta have the uncomfortable yet authentic conversations with your friends. If you want to know if you're connected to an abuser, gain peoples' trust. No one will open up to you unless they trust you first. Talk with your friends. Look out for your friends. Intervene when you see something that isn't okay.

Forrest Gump voice "And that's all I have to say about that."

CHAPTER SIXTEEN

GEEKY MOM REVIEW: NERDY BABY STUFF FROM OMA'S GOODIES

Here's a feel-good review on geeky baby items that I tried out on my real life baby. Messes were made in the process, but that's just a day in the life of parenting.

Disclaimer: I reached out to the ladies of Oma's Goodies to see if they would let me try their product in exchange for my honest review. I wasn't paid for this, so, uh, yeah. Honesty and whatnot.

The people want to know, "what's the point of you reviewing geeky baby stuff for geeky mommies?"

Well, I will give you two scenarios:

1. Maybe you're a first-time Geeky Mom. You can't wait to show off your Death Star-shaped belly and plan to use your maternity leave browsing cute baby stuff on Etsy. The reality is: you'll be too full of love, overwhelmed, sleep deprived, and maybe a little smelly (cause let's face it, showers are a world-class luxury those first few months) with no energy to open a browser. So wouldn't it be nice if your old pal

Quinzel tested it out for you? That could buy
you a precious thirty minutes of sleep.

2. Or let's say you don't have kids. And you want
   to buy things for your friends that are as useful
   as they are adorable. Unfortunately, sometimes
   you just get one or the other. And how the heck
   would you know for sure when you don't have
   any babies to test it on?

One look through Oma's Goodies Etsy shop and you
will be wishing for septuplets, 'cause you will want to dress
all of your offspring in their adorable geeky babywear.

The pattern I got was Minions and it was awfully cute.
The stitching on all of the items was very professionally
done. The opposite side of the fabric was absorbent and
soft.

So if you're looking for cute fandom stuff. You're in the
right place. But, like how we question all cute things, is it
useful?

Because here's the thing. Your baby is going to spit up
A LOT. Then they are going to drool A LOT MORE. So
you would get lucky if your cutesy nerdy baby stuff lasted
through one photo. Again, this is not the case with Oma's
Goodies. This stuff is useful annnndd cute.

The burp cloth is the perfect size while the bib is a little
small triangle shape. At first, I was a bit worried about
that, but as it turns out, it was perfect.

The material on the back of the burp cloth and bib
remind me of those ShamWow commercials because I'm
telling you, it gets up everything. There was a pretty epic
spit-up that somehow missed the bib completely and ended
up on the floor. I was able to soak it all up just using
the bib!

Lastly, the Minions tie is just darn cute. It ended up in

Bby-8's mouth several times, so I'm just going to take that as he loves it too.

So if you're a mom or buying a gift for a mom, Oma's Goodies is the way to go. Not only is it cute and useful, the prices are really affordable. I am probably going to return myself and get the Star Wars set.

Check out Oma's Goodies Facebook page and also their Etsy shop. And if you're a new mom reading this, for the love of Pete, hand that baby off and get some sleep.

CHAPTER SEVENTEEN

GEEKY MOM REVIEW: EASY GEEKY NAILS BY ESPIONAGE COSMETICS

A s a new mom, I wanted to know if nail wraps would be feasible with, say, cleaning bottles and spit up. So I felt it was necessary to conduct a review and do a little self-care for myself at the same time. Full review is below.

Disclaimer: on my search for nerdy products to make my hectic mom life a little easier, the ladies at Espionage Cosmetics were kind enough to send me their nail wraps to try in exchange for an honest review. They didn't pay me and all of the following is my truth.

This ain't yo' regular stick on nails!

For geeky girls like us, we want to have more than solid colors and chevron patterns. No one else will have something like Sonic The Hedgehog nail wraps any time soon. We are the oddballs of the earth, and we wear it proud! And Espionage Cosmetics helps you to wear that oddball geekery right on your nails.

That being said, I am a mom, a new mom at that. I bite my nails, I wash bottles constantly, and... let's not get started on diaper changes. But my baby, Bby-8, is still the coolest. Even if I have to sacrifice my geeky fashion.

Yeah, I ain't seen a nail polish bottle in... I'm not sure,

sometime last year? Thing is, you can probably get a few strokes of polish on your nails as a new mom, but being ready at a moment's notice with a tiny baby meant that drying time was a thing of the past.

But I STILL want to look nice sometimes and just dress a little more...me. I freely admit I am not an adult. Age-wise, yes, I am in my thirties. But I am also showing up in Pac Man leggings and band tees. I like bright colors and I make soccer moms roll their eyes.

So, I stumbled upon Espionage Cosmetics at the beginning of my pregnancy. And, yeah, I was sold then. But shortly after clicking on it, that good ol' morning sickness kicked in and it was a distant memory.

But I have been given a second chance to try out these nails for myself and I am going to share with you my findings. Are the designs super cool? Are they easy to put on? How much can they withstand? Are the ladies of Espionage Cosmetics super cool? Keep reading on for my review.

<u>"Okay, Quinzel, How Do They Look Tho?"</u>
The designs are awesome. They have something for every kind of geek. From gamers to book nerds and even fans of grilled cheese, there's something for every kind of geeky girl. If I had unlimited funds, I'd most definitely get one of each (yes, even the grilled cheese one).

LISTEN, don't be silly like me and forget to peel the clear backing off the front. It makes a HUGE difference in the nerdy nail wraps looking more like polish instead of like a sticker.

. . .

"I Am Also a Geeky Mom and I Ain't Got That Much Time To Be Doing Nails."

Girl, me neither! Again I was lucky if I could get one nail painted before I had to attend to Bby-8. Thing is, these wraps are quick, easy, and you don't even have to apply heat to them! I do recommend using a top coat to get a little more last out of it, but again, if time is a factor, you'll be okay without it.

"Does It At Least Outlast A Few Sleepless Nights? What Day Is it?"

I have....no idea what day it is, so I am going to deflect by telling you about how long it lasts. On the packaging, it says it can last up to two weeks. And since my maintenance has sorta plummeted, I can deal with not having to think about my nails for two weeks.

The thing is, as a Geeky Mom, I spend a lot of time washing bottles, and I mean, water and adhesives just don't mix. So as amazing as they are, at this stage in my life, they only make it about a week. On the plus side, I can't even get nail polish to last over twenty-four hours so...I mean that ain't so bad.

So... Should I Do the Thing?

If "the thing" is buy them, then yes, absolutely. Open a new tab on your browser. Do it now! I wouldn't endorse a product I wouldn't buy myself, so let's wait for this paycheck to drop and see what happens.

*= I mean; I'm not reviewing humans because that would be...idk? But I can assure you, you would want to be BFFs with these ladies in real life.

CHAPTER EIGHTEEN

PHILOSOFHER REVIEW: CUTE, COMFY, AND SATISFYING

I received this black "Wakanda-ish" shirt and onesie in exchange for an honest review. These are my honest thoughts (but spoiler alert, it's pretty great, y'all)

I feel like we discussed this on the podcast at some point (the Captain Marvel roundtable_episode of the podcast of all places) but one of the biggest pet peeves of mine is that there is hardly any Black Panther merchandise around. As much as I love Black Panther, I am sure that I could fund an entire Disney project, should they just give me what I friggin' want.

So imagine my surprise at showing up at WakandaCon and seeing this incredible Wakanda-ish shirt. And I completely lost it when I saw the Baby-ish onesie.

Before I get deep into this review, let me tell you a little bit about *Philosofher: The Love and Life of Her*. One look at the site and you'll be drawn in by the eye-catching apparel. Concitta, the genius behind *Philosofher*, also does event branding, wedding invitations, and more. She is a well-rounded creative.

According to the site (because I cannot do this amazing level of writing justice), this is *Philosofher's* story:

With intent, Philosofher is a collection of apparel, stationery, novelties, and such, curated to celebrate the life of, the love of, creatives and women - "...from [their] hair follicles to [their] toenails," - Jill Scott.

The selection of each item, the quotes penned or borrowed, the custom designs, and everything in between are all made possible with creative energy, passion, and detailed attention.

Embracing the laissez-faire and soul-snatching energy of New Orleans and the brazen, charming spirit of Chicago, Philosofher is what happens when the creativity of two cities collide and merge...

Simply, lagniappe.

First things first, I'm a plus-size gal. So with almost any clothes I wear, I find myself very disappointed to find they have nothing in my size. Pictured below, the Wakanda-ish shirt is in an XL and very roomy, I tucked it in to give it a fitted appearance, but the XL fit is AMAZING. Not too tight, not too big. I usually wear a 2X in shirts due to an abundance of boob-age. So this was an absolute win.

I live in an area where not many people get Black Panther or Black-ish references, but I still got a lot of compliments on it anyway.

The one who got the biggest compliments was my little Bb-y 8. He rocked that onesie like the model he is. The only thing he didn't like? The tag in the back. But it's an easy solution to cut the tag if needed. I've had to do it with A LOT of his clothes.

In case you couldn't tell, I love this company. The shirts are comfy. The sizing is dope, and it's cute as heck. Ten-out-of-ten would recommend.

What do you guys think? Think you'll head over to *Philosofher: The Love and Life of Her* and buy?

CHAPTER NINETEEN

QUICK QUINZEL FAMILY SNIPPETS

A s the sharks say in *Finding Nemo*, "Fish are friends, not food." That doesn't really make sense for this section does it? Neither does family sometimes. Enjoy some snippets about some hard, sometimes fun, lessons that I've learned about family.

Challenges You Will Unlock in Your First Year of Parenting

- Changing A Diaper (successfully) In The Dark - Now there will be many times you will change a diaper in the dark and not do it successfully. Putting it on backwards, not fastening correctly (I blame that on the sleep deprivation), and not changing fast enough are all rookie mistakes that can (usually) be avoided in the light.

- It's Too Quiet!! Panic! - OMG is he breathing? He's been asleep for longer than twenty minutes…but I don't want to wake him…but now I'm too afraid to sleep.

- Slapping a Stranger into Next Week - I am not advocating for you to fight strangers to unlock your parental achievement award here. But when your Mama Bear instincts kicks into high gear, you'll get what I mean.

- Spit Up in Your Hair - Bonus if you had a work meeting first thing in the morning.
- Crying When They Get Their First Shots - Idk why this hurt my feelings so much.
- Crying When They Finally Say Mama - Mine said Dada for what felt like a good century before he said, "Mama" and I was completely overcome with joy.

Best TV Families

- *Family Matters* - Carl Winslow was a cop who talked to his kids softly. Never demeaned them or beat them. In fact, I remember thinking it was weird that he never spanked his kids. Still the way that him and Mama Winslow ran their household was nice to little Quinzel.
- *Fresh Prince of Bel Air* - When I was younger, I just wanted to live in that huge, awesome house. But seeing Uncle Phil and Aunt Viv show so much love to their kids, and even their addition, Will, was enough for me to want that kind of family someday.
- *Black Panther* - Shuri and T'challa have the best sibling relationship ever. They joke and laugh and have infinite respect for one another. T'Challa is protective but understands that Shuri can hold her own in the lab. And I loved watching every minute of it onscreen.

Best Moments from My Wedding

- The Centerpieces: We decided to have board games that we already owned as centerpieces. I just remember attending so many weddings and being bored out of my mind when the couple would take their photos. I wish that I had something to do during that downtime. Thus, the idea of having board games as centerpieces was born.
- Rock, Paper, Scissors: We played Rock, Paper, Scissors to see who got to say their vows first.
- First Dance: Our first dance was actually playing Just Dance. We danced to "Single Ladies" by Beyonce. We were playing against each other and he noticed I was losing because the camera couldn't detect my leg movements with my wedding dress. So he stopped dancing so I could win. What a sweetheart!
- The Honeymoon: It took place at a convention center where a comic convention was going on at the time. I walked into the hotel lobby in my wedding dress and everyone complimented my "cosplay."
- My shoes: I've never been great at walking in heels, and I didn't really see any flats that I liked. So I bought a five dollar pair of white tennis shoes from Walmart and paid a friend to paint Wonder Woman on them. She even got gold shoelaces to look like gold lassoes. To this day, one of my favorite pair of shoes.

IN SICKNESS AND HEALTH

CHAPTER TWENTY

THE MESS THAT IS MS

Hi! My name is Quinzel, and I have MS. I'm also a mess XD.

I love how closely MS and "a mess" sound. Because that's exactly what my life became when I received that diagnosis.

But much like that pile of laundry that always seems to grow, it's a mess that needs maintaining. I can ignore it and put it aside as week by week the pile grows, or I can just say "I put away laundry on Wednesdays" and accept that this is a part of my life now.

Let me back up a bit for those who don't know about MS. MS stands for Multiple Sclerosis and it means multiple scarring on the brain.

That sounds…terrifying I'm sure. More so that there is no cure and doctors don't know what causes it.

I'm going to just hop in here and tell you that Multiple Sclerosis is not a death sentence. It's more of a life sentence with medicine. But definitely not fatal in most cases and in mine.

Getting over the fact that it's not fatal, but knowing that

it does not come with a cure or reason, here's what actually occurs in the brain.

Your nerves have these little protective covers called myelin. Think of how a cord works, you don't see the actual electric part. That plastic cover, that's myelin.

Much like an autoimmune disease, your body is attacking itself, thinking that ALL the things are bad, including the good ol' protective covering of myelin.

So what happens if you take the protective plastic off the cord? It's exposed and open for damage. Imagine pouring water on that with the protective coating off. You're about to not have a good time.

The breakdown of the myelin opens you up for a world of problems, depending on where they hit.

For me, it was my optic nerve behind my right eye. I had noticed that I couldn't see clearly on the right side. I could sort of see around the edges, but at times my vision was just blurry. It started off easy to ignore, like looking through a heavily rained on windshield. But then my husband noticed I had walked right past him in public. I waved off his concerns as "I'm fine, maybe I just need glasses and I'll get around to it anyway."

It was a weird thing; I was almost thirty years old but had always passed all of my eye exams. Deep down I knew it was something much bigger.

You know how people say you shouldn't google your symptoms? Take it from me, not only do I regret doing this, but not one of them turned out to be correct. I got a lot of results saying glaucoma, a few that signaled early-onset blindness, and at least two results that pointed to an aggressive, deadly form of cancer.

I was done.

The searches were overwhelming and I didn't want to know more. I silently protested to myself *no more!* This could just be my little secret and I could take it to the grave.

I couldn't handle a diagnosis.

One night, my husband did something he rarely does, he cried. Not a full-on ugly cry like I often do. But, at night when we lay in bed and I declined his request to find out what was going on with my eyesight, I heard a break in his voice.

"I just want to catch this early," he told me.

He was right. There was a large chance that this wasn't fatal. But there was an even larger chance that if we didn't figure this out now, we would have bigger consequences in the future.

Don't tell him I told you this, but he was right.

He thought it was best to start with the eye doctor. He sat in the waiting room while I went to the back for my exam.

Did I mention I hate getting my eyes touched? I knew, since I was a child, if anyone was going to put drops in my eyes, I had to sit on my hands, because instinctively, I keep pushing them away. The eye drops took forever. He asked me to call out the letters I could see on my left and my right. On my left side, I saw one huge black E. And on my right, just white.

More clicks "and on the right?" the doctor would say.

"Nothing, just white."

He took a look in my eye and then said "okay" under his breath. While he pulled his stool closer to me, I imagined myself wearing cute black cat eye glasses because I clearly needed them.

He put his hands in his lap and tried his hardest to look in my direction, but at times he looked down, unsure.

"You have an inflamed nerve behind your eye," he

said. There was more. He gave me a very vague explanation.

But I wasn't getting glasses today. I was being sent to the Emergency Room.

I panicked. "I don't…what's going on?" I asked him.

And then everything was a blur. I was at home, holding my ER transfer paperwork and shaking. My husband told me it's going to be okay, just pack an overnight bag in case we get admitted.

And I lost it.

Crying while holding a folded pair of fuzzy pajamas, what echoed in my mind was one of the last things that my mother told me. "You think you can make it out here without us? Fine!"

I was still sobbing as I put on my hospital gown. My husband asked softly, "Do you want me to call your mom?"

"No!" I told him, not yelling, but boldly and clear. In my mind, I reflected on all the times that my mom would visit a family in the hospital. Family would gleefully proclaim how God always steps in to bring family together.

Seeing that smug look of "I knew you would need me" when I was at my weakest was enough to stop my tears. I sat up straight and told him "No, I can face this without her."

They admitted me to the hospital and it was a week of Hell, but also a week of joy and love. There in the ER waiting room, the doctor tried to stick a long needle in my back twice. I sat on the edge of the bed, my body hunched over a table. The further the needle went in, the more nerves he hit. Pain shot up in different areas of my body. It took everything in me to stay still. My tears pooled at the edge of the table both times.

They got me to a room and hooked me up to a bag of steroids. That week was a constant rotation of friends.

Even the nurses became my friends. We played card games and had good conversation. We even laughed so loudly that the nurses told us, with smiles on their faces, to be a little quieter.

I was afraid of what the outcome would be, but this was an energy of love and laughter.

The first two needles didn't take, so after getting an MRI the day before, I was now taken to a room to get a lumbar puncture. This procedure, they stick a big needle up your spine and draw out the fluid. This will show the bands of myelin in your spinal fluid (from being ate up like I told you earlier). Most people have 1-2 bands. I had 10.

In the room, I was nervous after having this done twice unsuccessfully. The nurse was a kind, heavy set man, but I only saw his eyes as he was completely covered and scrubbed in. They had me lay on my stomach so it was a tad easier not to move.

"I know it's painful, but you're doing great," he told me. I couldn't move my hands to wipe away my tears of pain, and he would gently dab my cheeks to catch my tears.

I don't even know his name. Wherever you are, thank you. I'll never forget that level of compassion.

It would be a few more days until I was released to go home. Then a few days after that, I got the results of the MRI and Lumbar Puncture.

"You have multiple sclerosis."

I cried right there in my bathroom with my husband. Still unsure of what this disease means.

Disease, I have a disease.

Thoughts began to creep in my head of what my family told me. "You can't do this on your own, you'll come crawling back."

And almost instantly, I told myself *no.*

I remembered that moment in the ER. The very moment I said that I wasn't going to lean on people who hurt me and make them feel justified in the pain they inflicted on me.

I wasn't going to let guilt and shame eat me up anymore. And I wasn't going to accept this disease as a punishment.

I was going to handle it. And I was going to face it.

I never in a million years thought that this would be something that I would have to deal with, but just like I told you guys earlier, MS is a mess. And it's a mess to be managed.

Three times a week, I take a shot. I absolutely hate it. I even hated flu shots.

The dread of it being a Shot Day used to bother me all day. The biggest side effect is that it gave you flu-like symptoms which is... great? But it usually resulted in just feeling tired and having muscle aches.

Still, this is the life sentence that I was dealt. It's a mess of clean laundry that needs to be folded and dealt with every week.

But, having clothes isn't so bad, is it?

So I manage. I deal with the mess of MS as it comes at me. I have this amazing support system called my family. They give me the strength to figure out each day.

And each day, I'll keep fighting. I can face this.

So if you like research and need to know more about MS, The National Multiple Sclerosis Society and The Multiple Sclerosis Association of America are two great organizations that have lots of information.

And without further ado, here are some articles that are pretty... sick, if I do say so myself. *dodges tomatoes thrown on the stage*

CHAPTER TWENTY-ONE

I HATE USING MY CANE: HERE'S WHY

I woke up Monday morning to many pictures on my feed of Selma Blair wearing a gorgeous dress. What I didn't understand at first was why so many people were tagging me in it.

She has a cane. She has multiple sclerosis. Just like me.

I've discussed many times on the blog and on the podcast that I have MS. Shocker, right? First response I always get it that I don't LOOK sick.

Gee thanks, where's my Emmy?

But I conquer a whole level of commentary once I leave the house with my cane. And I hate it. I'm glad that Selma showed us that you don't need to put away your dreams because of your diagnosis. But I need to take the time to let you know that people can say some shitty things when they see you have a cane.

Do I need my cane all the time? *No.* Should I be using it more often? *...yes*, but to be quite honest, I don't use it as much as I need to. As I get bombarded with these variation of comments.

. . .

"You're too young to use a cane!"

While I want to give them a pass because, as I discussed on the podcast, I look and dress like I am sixteen years old, after hearing it for the 545,640,590,123,509th time, it gets old...older than I am BUT THAT'S NOT THE POINT!!

Don't remind me that I can't run around here like my peers, cane free. And don't invalidate my struggle because I don't LOOK the way you want my sick ass to look.

"What's that thing even for anyway?"

The weirdest thing about this comment is that they know damn well that it's a cane and they know damn well I am using it to walk. What they want is to open the door for me to give them more information. And if you're an acquaintance, a co-worker, or just a goddamned stranger, I don't owe you an explanation.

"But you were walking yesterday!"

Ohhhh, that last one. Yes, I can walk without a cane. I still have legs. They aren't the most functional. But they are capable of short distances. I get to decide what days I need my cane and what days I don't. Deal with it.

My Best Comebacks

You need a good set of coping skills to deal with these comments. Fortunately, I have a smart mouth. So here's some of the comebacks I have to the questions I get.

- "What are you doing with a cane?" Minding my own business, mind yours.

- "Why do you have that?" It's a fashion accessory, don't you know? It's totally in.
- "You're too young for a __" And you've been around long enough to know that what you're saying is rude. Stop it!
- "I think you're faking being sick." On the contrary, I fake being well.

Maybe Selma Blair using her cane is a good thing. Maybe a few well-meaning people will choose their words more carefully before speaking.

And maybe, just maybe, they will start making more fashionable canes. One to match every outfit? Nerdy canes? Yes, please.

CHAPTER TWENTY-TWO

COMICS AND CHRONIC ILLNESS: HOW AVA FROM ANT-MAN AND THE WASP PERFECTLY DESCRIBED MY INVISIBLE SYMPTOMS

H i, I'm Quinzel. I have Multiple Sclerosis.
"Hi, Quinzel" my imaginary audience says, "we don't believe you"

While hurtful, it's understandable. I fall under the category of people who don't look sick. It's why they call it an invisible illness.

Multiple sclerosis, or MS as it's shortened, is a snowflake disease, meaning symptoms can be different for everybody. Do we know why? No. Is there a cure? Also, no.

One of the hardest things about my disease is explaining to people what it feels like daily for me. Aside from telling them that getting off my medication won't actually make me feel better and eating a bunch of oranges won't cure it, I also have the worst time trying to explain how I feel.

some Ant-Man and the Wasp spoilers ahead

Then I went to see *Ant-Man and the Wasp*. We were introduced to the character Ghost, known as Ava, who is constantly phasing in and out while experiencing a lot of pain. Long story short, the lab explosion that killed her parents didn't kill her, it just fucked her up to holy hell.

There's a symptom that I have that I can't describe in one word. But Ava's phasing shows it pretty well. It's this weird out of body experience like I'm jumping from one scene to another. It makes me feel as if I'm about to pass out.

The second is the pain. The constant pain. When you're in pain, minutes feel like hours, hours feel like days. While there is a level of pain I can deal with on a daily basis and still function, once I've passed that level, it's all over.

Just like Ava, I am always in pain. Always.

So, I get it. Being so close to not being in pain every day and you tell me we *can't do the thing*? Most people will never get to experience that level of desperation. It's a feeling where you will do absolutely anything to get rid of the pain. Living in constant pain robs you of the ability to have any sort of chill. Hell, it robs you of the ability to just live.

So, I get it. Do I agree with her plans? Mostly no, but I understand. To phase every day, almost like a slow-burning glitch, on top of being in pain sucks to the highest level. All you can do is wait to crawl into bed only to do it all over again.

So now that I've opened myself up to you guys, I'm curious what your lives are like. Any of you deal with a chronic illness, disability, or undiagnosed "why Lord?" level of pain? Have you seen it represented in media in an accurate way? Would you like MORE representation?

CHAPTER TWENTY-THREE

QUINZEL SICK DAY STREAMING: CHECK OUT WHAT I'M WATCHING

Can I just tell y'all how much I NEVER wanna see another hospital again? If you've been following our Instagram @geekygirlguide, I've been sick, stuck in a hospital room and ultimately getting *gasp* surgery. Now that I'm released, I'm confined to Netflix. So I thought I'd give you guys a rundown of what I have been watching.

Just so you know, I avoided *Bird Box* completely. I loved the memes, but I just feel like I'm not going to watch it and I am going to be stubborn about it. Going forward, you won't hear s#!t from me about *Bird Box*.

100% Hotter (Netflix)

I needed a show where I didn't have to think. Something I could conk out on pain meds and still follow what was going on once I woke up. My friend recommended this show and said it was not as shaming as a certain-show-on-TLC-is/was. She also told me that the stylists even worked to keep them within their original look. Cool! Sold.

I'd recommend it because it's not a farm mill pushing out the same end result just on different people. The stylists seem to really cater to each individual and their personal style. And it's given me some ideas as to what to do with my own style that keeps constantly changing.

I Feel Bad (Hulu)

This show came up randomly after I dozed off for a bit, and honestly, it was a happy little accident. What could have just been another white show about white problems turned out to be this cool, really authentically diverse show. Meds or not, this was a pretty entertaining show.

She frigging works for a fictional gaming company. *jealous*

(My husband would like to tell you all that this show is essentially _Black-ish_ with a few differences. There, honey, I told them.)

Tidying Up with Marie Kondo (Netflix)

This show got a lot of hate that I only noticed after I finished it. I gotta be honest here. This isn't going to be a hate review; I really liked this show. I felt like it was very different from other _throw out your clutter_ shows in that it didn't emphasize shaming each person. I felt like each person was relatable in their own way, and I didn't get lost in sitting on my couch like "Ahhhh, at least I'm NOT AS MESSY AS YOU!!!" because truth is, I struggle with laundry too. And if my broke ass had the money, I'd absolutely pay someone to do it and put it away.

Loved the black family because they were already so full of joy and I felt like Marie participated in that joy.

They also just seemed like a really sweet, kind family, and they were very refreshing to watch.

I like when she entered each house that she bowed. It showed a lot of respect like "hey, I get this is your house and I'm just a visitor. I'm here to help, not to judge."

Did I mention I LOVED how there was no suggestions to go buy more things to be more organized? That she used what they already had? Ahhh, glorious!

The real question is: when I am recovered from my surgery, am I going to go through *my* junk? Uhhhh, I can't really think about that right now.

Grown-Ish (Hulu)

I watched the first season…actually, last time I was in the hospital XD. I feel like I get a sick satisfaction from Zoey fucking up her early college experience. But that's 'cause we ALLLLL been there. It's kind of comforting knowing someone as gorgeous as her is overthinking as much as the rest of us. Especially over relationships. I mean, I'm married now, but, GOD, DATING WAS SUCH A PAIN. *Does he like me? Does he not? Is he texting someone else? Is he thinking about Pringles?* I don't miss those days.

I will say that my hair did not look as good as hers does in college. I lived in bandanas and PJs. 'Cause screw looking pretty when I'm living on two hours of sleep. But, you do you, Zoey.

So those have been my binges so far. Hopefully, I'll get off this damn couch soon. What are you guys watching right now?

CHAPTER TWENTY-FOUR

QUINZEL'S SICK LIST

Hey, sometimes when I'm not feeling well, I can't think in full sentences. I can only think in lists and bullet points. Here's what I need you to do next:

- Read this
- Enjoy!

Must Haves for an Overnight Hospital Bag

- Hair ties: Do not try to shuffle your butt down to the gift shop simply because you're tired of trying to find new, inventive ways to pull your hair back. Just make sure to have a few handy, because after being poked and prodded, you are going to want ONE less thing bugging you.
- Socks: Hospitals are really just large freezers. Which is a lot better than it being a furnace. But after having a nurse bring me warm blanket after warm blanket, what would help me is keeping my feet warm first. Hospital socks

are fine, but if you keep a nice, fuzzy warm pair of socks in your bag, you'll thank yourself for it later.

- Soft blanket: because the nurses may not appreciate you hoarding all of the warm blankets, even though you're freezing. Bring an extra pillow for comfort too.

- Comfy pajamas: Hospital gowns get old after a while. Thing is, you don't even realize how much it's affecting your mood until you put on your own comfy clothes. Pick something like pajamas. Don't make the mistake of packing jeans and a t shirt and then you're unable to get comfortable.

- Coloring book or word puzzle: Here's the thing about hospitals. It's a big waiting game. Waiting for surgery, waiting to see the doctor, waiting to see if you can be discharged today and so on. You need something to pass the time, because the ticking of the big, round wall clock will drive you crazy.

- Real clothes to go home in: I have always felt the transition from hospital to home is much easier if I am in *real people* clothes on the drive home.

- Headphones: It's courteous to be respectful of any neighbors nearby or not play things loud enough to be heard all the way over in the nurses' station. But aside from that, you will want something to drown out the sound of constant beeping.

- Phone Charger: This is the most important thing and I almost always forget it each time. My first weeklong hospital stay, I was so shocked by the news that something might be wrong with me, I couldn't even think what I needed to pack. Luckily, my significant other was able to run back home and get my cords. But, man, having your phone either as a way to contact people or just simply a means of entertainment can go a long way. Especially when you aren't quite sure of the timeline that they will release you.

Three Things No Chronically Ill Person Ever Wants to Hear

- "You Don't Look Sick" It's hard to hear because what I am actually hearing is "are you SURE you're sick?" and the answer is yes, a thousand times yes. I know better than someone who I just met.
- "Have You Tried…" - The first thousand times I heard it, I really wanted to believe and try all the things. But failed attempt after failed attempt, this question gets to you. Yes, I have tried Yoga, losing weight, paleo, and whatever else you might suggest. Which brings me to my next point.
- "Medicine Is Bad for You" - I don't know how to put this lightly, it is highly rude and a bit unethical to suggest that someone go off their medicine when you are not a doctor. Not to mention, it's dangerous advice. Just don't do it. People have died this way. Leave 'em alone.

How to Make the Best Of Your Illness When You're In It For Life

- Pain Playlist - Music has helped me get through those really hard moments of having a chronic illness. Whether it's a bad flare up day or I'm just not having the energy to do anything else, music is a great relaxer. I have a pain playlist that I switch up every so often with music that's really calming to me.
- Decorate Your Mobility Aids - I have a cane that I put stickers on. I have a friend who painted hers like The Winter Solider from *The Avengers.* I also have compression gloves for my hands with little duckies on them. You can't imagine how much my mood lifts up when I look down and see I have little ducky hands.
- You Can't Be Positive All of the Time - recognizing this is what will keep you sane. Yes, there are many things to be grateful for. And yes, you are a strong and worthy individual despite your illness. And sometimes, you feel sad. Maybe you even feel like crying. The best gift that you can give yourself in this life is allowing yourself to be sad when you need it.

Things to Do While You Are Waiting in The MRI Machine

- Counting the number of clicks - For me personally, this gets boring real fast. But for someone else, counting the number of clicks might be soothing. So I included it

- Try to create a new, hit song - Sometimes those clicks turn into beats and I like to pretend I'm in a Writers Room in an LA studio trying to find different rhythms for the new, next, hit song. Play it again, brother!

- Listen to music - this is the obvious one. One thing I kind of look forward to is the nurse asking me to pick my station. I'm inclined to pick something relaxing, but I try to pick something loud and fast enough to drown out the sound of the MRI.

- Imagine you are working in a construction zone - Just working a live, long day. Working up a sweat. Eating my lunch while sitting on a high beam above the city. This is the life.

- Sleep - I know, it's crazy to think you could actually sleep in there. My first MRI after I had Bby-8 was a dream. I was very sleep deprived and I got two hours of uninterrupted sleep. It was glorious.

COSPLAY AND GAMING
THE QUINZEL WAY

CHAPTER TWENTY-FIVE

COSPLAY AND SOME SERIOUS STUFF TOO

The funny thing about me is that I was cosplaying before I knew what cosplay was.

For those new to the term cosplay, it's a combination of the words *costume* and *play*. It's basically Halloween everyday, minus the candy. I've always wanted to dress up outside of that holiday.

When I was younger, I loved to play dress up. Halloween was my favorite holiday. And just like any other young girl in the '90's, I wanted to dress-up as a Disney princess.

I remember telling a group of friends that I wanted to be Cinderella for Halloween.

"You can't be Cinderella," one of the girls sneered at me, "you're black."

I was in second grade at the time, So, just to give you an idea, this was before Rodgers and Hammerstein's *Cinderella* which starred Brandy Norwood at Cinderella. All we had at the time was the blonde, animated Cinderella. Me with my medium brown skin and two big puffy pony tails wasn't princess-y enough for them. Though this wasn't my first time being typecast for being black, it wouldn't be the last. Throughout my life, I would be told to be Scary Spice instead of Baby Spice or to be Moesha instead of Britney Spears.

I wanted a world where my imagination didn't have limits, where I could be characters and I wasn't limited by my skin color. But in the beginning of my geek journey, cosplay felt like a world of no.

Once I was well into adulthood, I began to discover the world of cosplay. I learned that I wasn't the only weirdo in the world who loved to play dress-up. I would learn a whole world of cosplayers.

I became equally impressed with folks who were also able to build their cosplays from scratch, as well as those who can put together items in a store.

Since I lack superior seamstress skills, I rely on shopping in thrift stores and having a sense of humor for putting together my cosplays. My absolute favorite cosplay that I have done was when I went as a Cards Against Humanity white card. The back of the card read the infamous "Cards Against Humanity" logo and the front of the card said "A sassy black woman."

It was fun for me to walk around in that cosplay, I got a lot of high fives that day, and let's be honest, it was funny.

But deep down, race is a big deal in the cosplay community. I've seen subtle things like someone calling someone the black version of whatever character to really big, hurtful things like drawing black cosplayers as monkeys.

If you've read up until this point, you know that I have a stake in being different. Once I learned that cosplay was a thing, I was all in. It was so sad to learn how people often attack cosplayers for merely existing. Honestly, no matter what you do, you can't escape it. People complain that you are too fat. People complain that you're too sexy. They even complain that you didn't portray a character accurately enough. It's almost as if there isn't a "play" in cosplay.

Why make a fun thing so hurtful? Why attack people because they are just having fun?

It takes me back to those Cinderella days, to being told I can't be Baby Spice at recess, to being placed in a box I never asked to be in.

Cosplay is a dream. It's a fun world where all of these characters we see on the big and small screen come together. It's a love like no other.

Whether you are costume ready or just rolling out of bed, here are some articles about cosplay. Enjoy!

CHAPTER TWENTY-SIX

COSPLAYER CONVOS: SUPPORTING STRONG
FRIENDS THE WAY THAT THEY SUPPORT YOU

I 'm working with a new concept here. A series of blog posts and interviews that I will call *Cosplayer Convos*.

I enjoy cosplay. I admire cosplayers. But I think we forget that the person behind the cosplay is...a person. We see them at conventions and follow them on social media and sometimes forget that these glorified humans are just...human. I believe that by sitting down and talking to them, we can all learn something new.

Thus, I present to you: *Cosplayer Convos*.

So, What Is a Strong Friend?

You know who they are. They are that go-to person on social media. They always know what to say. Or they're someone you consider to be an IRL (in real life) friend. They don't give a crap how your homophobic uncle feels about "that lifestyle" (this is not going to be the first time I go in on your uncle, #sorrynotsorry), they're going to fight the good fight anyway.

. . .

Bri @ Organizing Apocalyptic Fabrics @BrichibiTweets

"Queer content creator self-care tip: Don't dwell on the folks who turn their nose or roll their eyes when you say your work is queer. Use that energy to value the folks who appreciate what you're putting out into the universe."

Our strong friends save the day, without breaking a sweat or shedding a tear

But, where do our strong friends go when they need a strong friend? Who do they have when they need advice? Where is a shoulder when they need to cry?

I'm holding myself accountable, as I am the friend who is often in need. I have benefited from having strong friends swoop in and rebuild me, time and time again. As someone who was still building their support system, I was extremely thankful.

BUT...was I asking them how their day was going? Was I even calling them just to have fun or was I just expecting them to appear when my life was falling apart? Was I only prepared to tag them on Facebook when arguing social justice issues, like I was summoning a Pokémon with a higher CP than my own?

When I think of a strong friend, or just a strong person in general, my mind goes to one person. One of the strongest people I know is our fearless leader, owner, and admin of Geeky Girl Guide, Leslie. Remember that time she announced on the podcast that if you are being harassed and need someone, she's your girl? Yeah, she's the bomb. She has told people she will feast on their cracklings before. And dammit, she means it. Don't mess with her.

She's got an amazing heart and will defend you to the end. As I often am scared, short, and not the least bit intimidating, I admire her strength and her ability to always push back and to speak up for what is right. Leslie does not give a red cent f#$k what you think about her.

Wrapped in all of that strength is a human being, who is just as deserving of someone willing to tear someone apart for her as she is for others. Leslie deals with life just as much as my emotional ass does. And she deserves the support that she gives to all of us.

This post is about Briana of Brichibi Cosplays, but I'm dedicating this post to Leslie. Leslie: *You are strong, you are seen, and you are appreciated. Never stop being you.* <3.

Briana: The Strongest Woman You Will Ever Meet

Briana is a cosplayer that I've admired for years. Not just the ability to rock amazing cosplays (I think my favorite is a toss-up between Tiana and Wonder Woman) but to take up space in a way I hadn't seen before. Here she stood. Black. Fat. Queer. And magical.

Alongside the love of her life and longtime partner, Jessica (who is an amazing seamstress by the way), Briana seemed to have it all. But in spite of her successes, hateful people saw her and did what they did best. For every positive thought we had for Briana, there were twenty more people who were angrily typing on their keyboards letting us know in all caps how they couldn't stand her.

Briana was always overcoming. For every hateful comment, she had an equally positive one. It was always in a perfect way to shut them down. *She's got to be the strongest woman I will ever meet*, I often thought to myself.

There was something I didn't realize that was going on behind these posts. While I was reading them in real time, I was putting myself down thinking of how I would be *too sensitive* to deal with this if it was directed at me. I remember thinking Briana was *so strong*.

"I responded to every comment," Briana says about her social media posts at the beginning of her cosplay journey. I remembered this about her. I read them and admired her for being *so strong* despite the ongoing homophobic, fatphobic, and downright racist comments she received. *Sooooo strong*, and yet...

When her partner, Jessica, came home earlier that day, she noticed that Briana had been responding to each and every comment on Tumblr and told her to turn anonymous comments off. "I was like, 'I can't do that, I have to show people that if you get bullied, there's a person who can stand up and deal with it,'" Briana describes of that day.

Jessica persisted, pointing out that she had been on Tumblr all day responding to comments. She again told Briana she should turn anonymous comments off. Almost instantly, Briana felt a sense of relief. "It was this moment of 'oh my God, I'm allowed to walk away.'"

Waiting to Exhale: Are Your Strong Friends Holding Their Breath?

"I don't think people realize that the strong friend doesn't usually start out as being strong," Briana says.

"I'm very vocal about different issues, and I write about them and it's really great. But people don't understand how much that weighs down on you because most of us are pulling from personal experiences."

One thing we talked about is this iconic scene from *Waiting to Exhale. Yes, that one.* Where Angela Bassett's character Bernie burns the car of her cheating husband. It's a pretty memorable scene that left many people saying the '90s equivalent catchphrase of YASSSSS QUEEN.

Briana brings up a great point about this scene. "Everyone talks about how she burnt the car and, its badass, but before that, she sat in her room and cried and even after [that scene] she cried some more. That comes with the territory of being the strong friend..."

Forgetting that our strong friends have feelings and pain behind that strength is doing them a disservice. We believe tears and strength cannot coexist. That's the trap we fall into, believing our strong friends are exempt from the pain they're always saving us from.

Too Strong and Too Soft: A Confusing and Frustrating Paradox

"It's so frustrating because they don't want us to be vulnerable, but they don't want us to be too strong either," Briana says.

I can definitely see what she means by this. It's almost like we expect our strong friends to be strong within our parameters. It's like we tell them, *you need to be strong, but in a way that is beneficial to me* and this has to change.

"With the strong friend title, they forget about the friend part," Briana says, "and just focus on the strength part."

While this paradox can present itself in times of support, it can also present itself when your strong friend is being outspoken. Once they hit a nerve with someone, they're expected to pull back.

"I thought our friendship could withstand [insert topic]" is something that Briana often hears. Because she's often outspoken on these issues that often affect her personally, there seems to be this unspoken soft spot she hits with people. "I thought our friendship could withstand this" often translates to "I love it when you speak out, just not about me."

They're telling their strong friend on the surface that they hope their friendship could withstand differing politics, subtle racist tweets, and separating their friend from their sexuality. But what they're really saying is "I thought our friendship could stay beneficial to me and not disrupt my beliefs."

Whatever the case, this is exhausting. Whether the lack of support comes from not having the space to be vulnerable or only being heard under certain terms, we have to do better for our strong friends.

How to Support Your Strong Friends

It was difficult for Briana to be vulnerable, even just on social media. When expressing her feelings on Facebook, she got responses from people who said: "I don't know how to talk to you because you're *so strong*" (<----see, there's that saying again).

Briana describes how one of her friends showed how to be supportive in the right way "She was like 'I know you're busy and I'm busy but whenever you're free we can get together and watch anime'...that's all I wanted!"

It's not always about having the right advice or cuddling them when they cry. Sometimes your strong friend doesn't need advice or cuddles. Sometimes they just need a distraction, a neutral zone that they can build themselves up again. And that's okay.

"Don't just check on us when we're suffering...also be there when we're having a good day." Briana brings up a really good point about not just being there in trials or triumphs, but in those boring in-between moments as well. Invite them to lunch when nothing particularly exciting is going on. Ask them how they're holding up just because it's Wednesday. Draw them a picture because you know it will cheer them up.

"I Shouldn't Have to Defend Myself from YOUR Friends:" A Quiz

Small rant before we get to the quiz. One of my biggest peeves about Facebook is going through hoops to keep all of my content limited to only the people I want to see it. While I've made attempts at putting stricter privacy setting such as *Friends Only*, by some small loophole, a status you make could still be seen by your friend's Racist Uncle Twice Removed.

Briana said something that was really impactful, especially in regards to Facebook.

"I shouldn't have to defend myself from *your* friends."

Grab your pencils, guys, this is your Quinzel Quiz of the day.

Your strong friend posts something that your Racist Uncle sees ('cause the way Facebook sets up mutuals, it happens). Racist Uncle does what he does best, which means sending a profoundly hateful and misspelled lashing to your strong friend.

In this situation, do you:

A) Assume your strong friend will handle it because she's great at this kind of thing?

B) Let your uncle know that he shouldn't talk to your friend that way and why, thus putting a protective barrier between your strong friend and your racist uncle who still needs help setting up his iPad.

The answer is B. But oftentimes what plays out is A. It goes back to the assumption that this strong friend has *GOT IT* because they are vocal from these issues, so why should this be any different?

That line of thinking isn't supportive to your strong friends. It's one thing to defend yourself from strangers, but having people you consider friends who just leave you hanging puts strong friends in a position of not only having to fight their own battles but yours too. Next time this happens, tell your Racist Uncle to take a hike and buy him a dictionary for Christmas. Auto correct will thank you.

Final Thoughts

All I really want us to do is ask ourselves are we supporting our strong friends in a way that's equal in the way they support us? Are we giving them space to be vulnerable? Or are we contributing to a burnout?

I can't tell you the number of times that I faced something in my life that was really hard but didn't think of myself as a strong person because I faced it with tears streaming down my face. I get down on myself because I think both can't co-exist. But Briana reinforced for me that I can cry my eyes out for hours and still be strong.

Briana has lived a life of pain, loss, and frustration. But she has also chased her dreams, fell in love, and continues to influence and affect everyone she meets in a positive way.

Your strong friend is this beautiful, vulnerable individual who is a force to be reckoned with. They take their tears and often turn them into a shield, protecting others from the pain they've been through. Their voice is loud because they're often speaking for the timid and unheard.

To Briana, Leslie, and all of my strong friends:

You are wonderful.

You are appreciated.

You are heard.

And remember, no matter if you've done this for a while or are just starting out. You. Are. Cosplay.

CHAPTER TWENTY-SEVEN

COSPLAYER CONVOS: COSPLAYING OVER 30

O ne of the most infuriating things I hear (mostly at my day job) is "Quinzel, you STILL go to comic book conventions? You STILL play video games? You STILL dress up?"

Yes. Yes. And, in case this is your first time to the blog, yes?

There was a time when I was much, much younger (I'm talking high school-ish age here) where I worked hard to cover my nerd flag as much as possible, lest I'd be called out and embarrassed for it.

Fast forward to today, I let that go a LONG time ago. Once I accepted who I was, the comments bothered me a lot less. I am taking the time to do something that makes me happy. *And that isn't making fun of other people's interests, Carol.*

The comments still come through. On top of that, we put a HUGE emphasis on turning thirty years old and what it means. We cry and cry in our last moments of twenty, like thirty really changes things.

I am a firm believer that thirty is not the mile marker

for all of your life's accomplishments. Thirty is only the beginning.

That is one big reason why I really connected with Erica (Suga Bear Co) because it was so refreshing to meet someone so unbothered by age. Not only is she unbothered but, as I stated earlier, this is only the beginning of many new adventures for her.

"The biggest piece of advice I can give a cosplayer over thirty is don't be afraid to be you." Erica says, "If cosplaying is something you have always wanted to do, make it a bucket list item and get it out of the way. Age only means something if you decide it means something. It doesn't have to cost a ton of money or be exactly perfect. Get out of your head and just do it."

Erica is a cosplayer and talented seamstress. Known by Suga Bear Co, she's got a lot of life under her belt. That isn't to say age. I think one thing people get intimidated about starting to cosplay later in life is because they feel as though it strays away from the current life path that you've built.

Erica is living proof that at any point in life, you can press restart. She isn't just carelessly starting and stopping things, she's an inspiration that, at any point, you can redefine yourself and your goals. And this has earned her a fulfilled life.

She received her Associate degree at thirty, her bachelor's at thirty-two and her master's at thirty-six. If this isn't proof that your life isn't over at thirty, I don't know what is.

Erica had always loved fashion and initially wanted to be a fashion designer when she was younger. But unlike the notion that says you must decide what you want to do by the time you turn eighteen, Erica took the time to explore different career and degree options. Along with that, she worked full time, went to school full time, and also was raising a child.

Cosplay didn't come easy for this hardworking gal. She couldn't attend conventions at first because she couldn't get the time off work. She had worked in operations in hotels where weekend shifts were required. Instead of giving up on cosplay altogether, she fit it in by dressing up for birthday parties and special occasions.

"My first con experience was at C2E2 2018," Erica says. "Sounds weird since I've been a cosplayer for thirteen years, but between job schedules and cost, it was not a priority. I made it a priority last year, and I'm glad I did. I got to see what the hype was about and how extravagant the cosplays really could be. I was able to attend the panels for plus size cosplay and Costumers with a Cause. I think I did about 20,000 steps per day and, of course, was extremely tired. I even did a costume change one of the days. That experience also let me know that I didn't need to go to any con for an entire weekend unless there are things I'm participating in each day."

Since then, she has also attended (and judged cosplay at) Toys and CosplayCcon as well as both years of WakandaCon. WakandaCon is where we initially met and I wanted to know if she loved it as much as I had.

"I have loved my experiences at WakandaCon because we weren't the afterthought. People are looking to photograph you and talk with you, interview you, respect you, because the con is about you and your tribe and how we interact. I have met some wonderful people, and I hear people every time tell me how I've inspired them by something I said at a panel. You don't really get that at bigger cons where there is no real focus and you're in a crowd of people who may not be so welcoming."

As amazing and strong as Erica is, that doesn't mean

that she doesn't recognize that there can be negativity in the cosplay world. Not just toward age, but size and race as well

"Some of the negative comments I've seen towards other cosplayers is that they are too dark to play a character or said character isn't Black, so you have to do someone else. I've seen people tell some of my cosplay kids that they ruined a character for them because they didn't feel they were perfect or that they were too fat to be certain characters. I've seen people be called the n-word version or ghetto version of a character."

Erica recognizes that it can be hard for new cosplayers to deal with that level of negativity. "If I had gotten into cosplay when I was younger, I would have gotten out of it." Then smiles and tells me, "I'm secure in myself that I'm gonna check 'em and keep it moving…don't give them what they're looking for…"

The positive side of growing with age is that you also grow out of fucks to give. However, there is one negative aspect that we haven't covered, and it isn't what people think of you.

Spoiler alert: It's money.

I can attest that the biggest thing that prevents me from going to more cons and donning myself in more cosplays is money. More than what people say, 'cause what even are words? Money, it seems, will snatch your dreams a lot faster than hurtful words can.

"Money is a challenge in cosplay because even the cheapest cosplay will still probably cost you at least twenty dollars if you can get it all through the thrift. Let's also add in any make-up needs, wig or hair needs, shoes or boot covers, accessories, etc. Then add in the cost of actually attending cons. Because I am now on panels, my costs have started to be covered a bit (for some cons), but before that started, I had to pay for my tickets, hotels if necessary, parking, gas, etc. I also cosplay with my kid, so there's the added cost of all of that stuff for him as well. "

To deal with these burdens we learn, with age, that self-care is key. I totally understand being busy, but it's inspiring to know that with how busy Erica is, she still prioritizes the importance of self-care. Also, have I mentioned that she is a trained therapist who is starting Group Cosplay Therapy?

" Self-care is a must for me. Being a therapist, I teach self-care to my clients so that they know this is a need and not a want. I also teach them what self-care includes because many people think it's massages, bubble baths, and shopping sprees. Self-care is also spending time doing things you love and with people you love. Cosplay is definitely a self-care, both making it and wearing it at the con or other events. Sewing, dancing, drawing, painting, and listening to music are also part of my self-care routine. Spending quality time with my kids watching our favorite anime or movies is also huge. Hanging out with my friends and family is always a fun time."

Erica proves that with everything you have to balance: school, kids, full-time job, that cosplay is possible if you want it to be possible. Just take the strength you have used in all of your other life situations and apply it to something you would have fun doing.

Push yourself out of your comfort zone (and other peoples' comfort zones) and shine.

Are you a cosplayer over thirty? What challenges have you experienced? What are some of the most fun or amazing experiences that you have had with cosplay?

CHAPTER TWENTY-EIGHT

COSPLAY ON THE CHEAP: NAKA KON PANEL WITH FULLELVEN COSPLAY

While attending Naka Kon, I also attended a panel called Cosplay on the Cheap facilitated by FullElven Cosplay and learned many tips and tricks on how to cosplay when my wallet was feeling pretty light.

Something I love: seeing cosplayers at conventions, admiring their handiwork, and swearing to myself that I'm gonna give it a go.

Something I hate: being too broke to try.

What's that saying I used to hear growing up? "You can't have champagne dreams on a bologna budget."

When it crossed my mind to try my hand at cosplay, I was filled with *I could never* and *who is financing this cosplay?* But attending the panel Cosplay Accessibility: Cosplay on the Cheap at Naka Kon removed that roadblock of *I'm just too dang broke.*

First Impressions

Running down the hall of the convention center, press

badge flying in the wind, I made it just in time for the panel to start.

The first thing I notice is Jace, aka FullElven Cosplay. There's something…calming about the room. Which sends me in an unnecessary panic. *Do I have a spot on my face? Is my skirt hiked up around my waist from all that running?*

Nah, this panel, as well as Jace, just gives off a chill atmosphere. Everything about this panel was amazingly well organized. There were slides created ahead of time, and Jace answered everyone's questions very well. It was done in a laid back, non-performative manner, and I think that opened it up for so many people to feel comfortable asking questions at the end. So, kudos to you for that, Jace!

There was also a wealth of information at this panel. Maybe I didn't know this info already because I'm not a seasoned cosplayer (unless you count the extensive plans I have in my head that I never execute). But by the end of the panel, I found cosplay builds *A LOT* less intimidating.

Here's just a few of the tips mentioned in the panel to make your cosplay cheaper:

Foam-Smithing

You ever want to build an entire suit of armor but you know purchasing armor costs money and food is necessary to survive? 'Cause…you need to obtain food with money…and armor costs…okay, okay, you're following me.

So Jace suggests either using foam or cardboard to build your armor. Both are really inexpensive, and foam can take shape really well.

Sewing

I have *very* **VERY** basic sewing skills. I know enough to be dangerous with attaching a button or fixing a hem, but that's about it, y'all. Some tips on sewing for those of us who need it:

- It's much cheaper to just buy a sewing machine that's used and tune it up in lieu of buying a brand new one. I would not have even thought to look in a thrift shop for one, so I'm glad that was put out there.
- There's also a way to get cheap sewing patterns (just wait for the sale, instead of buying at full price), but you can spend exactly $0.00 by using your own clothes and tracing them out to create your own pattern.
- You can also get cheap sewing supplies at Walmart.

Speaking of sales, Jace let us in on a secret (might be widely known, but I get excited over saving money so it's like a juicy secret to me).

Stack. Them. Coupons.

JOANN's allows you to use multiple coupons online and in store. Sign up for their emails, download the JOANN's store app, ~~give them an offering at their doorstep~~ and right there you've got several different coupon codes you can use on the same transaction.

With all that money you'll save at JOANN's, you could buy me...idk...candy or something.

Lighting

I normally would steer clear of any cosplay with lighting because I lacked the skill as much as the funding. But how did I forget that fairy lights were a thing? Most of them even come with a battery pack so no electrical experience needed.

Jace mentioned that if you want to make the lights appear brighter, using regular foil as backing works amazingly well.

Recommendations

During the Q&A session, a few questions came up and some GREAT recommendations.

- ELF makeup is just as good as expensive makeup and a LOT cheaper.
- An audience member recommended using Pros-Aid instead of Spirit Gum if you're allergic to latex. It's a medical grade adhesive.

Amazon and Ebay are cheap places to find cosplay supplies, HOWEVER, it varies from shop to shop. Quick Tip: *read the reviews. Trust accordingly.*

Gush Post on FullElvenCosplay Incoming in 3…2…

I know this is about the panel, but the panelist deserves quite a bit of praise. Any question about their expertise would be erased by looking through their Instagram @fullelven.cosplay.

I'm also going to be giving their Twitch channel a follow. I could definitely get behind watching their cosplay builds after a long day.

Jace has an impressive skill set. You can see through their cosplays that it takes a lot of time and effort to create. It's also quite inspiring to know that you don't have to sacrifice craftsmanship just because you're working within a budget.

This was just a short version of what was discussed in Cosplay Accessibility: Cosplay on the Cheap. Wanna know all the tips and tricks we discussed to save you money? Reach out to Jace on IG @fullelven.cosplay, and I'm sure they would be happy to offer any tips or tricks.

CHAPTER TWENTY-NINE

AN OPEN LETTER TO NAKA KON 2019 COSPLAY CONTESTANTS: YOUR PASSION GIVES US JOY

Cosplay has got to be one of the most fun and exciting hobbies to have. After all, half of the word is "play." But I think we forget that cosplay is also an art form. It's something that you build and pour all of your time, efforts, and heart into. When you present the product of your blood, sweat, and tears to the world, it's extremely validating to be rewarded for it.

Being a friend and fan to many cosplayers, I've witnessed the stress, the con-crunch, the pain, and the tears leading up to cosplay contests. It's a lot of work to prepare for.

But let me tell you, there wasn't a single one of you who didn't put a smile on my face.

- Cosplayer IG: @diana.the.great, winner of Best Beginner Craftsmanship at Naka Kon 2019.

If you were crying backstage, if you were stressed all week on your cosplay because it wouldn't be finished in time, if you *ever* felt you weren't good enough to compete in the first place…

I just want you to know, from where I'm sitting: I absolutely adore you.

- Cosplayer IG: @miss_pincushion, Winners of Best Master Overall at Naka Kon 2019.

You give me, and everyone else in the audience for that matter, a totally new reason to smile. To fall away from the ever-running list of adult responsibilities for a bit and soak in this fun and amazing artistry.

If you were nervous, it's okay! If you didn't win an award, know that you (yes, YOU) were recognized, not only for your hard work, but for the joy that you bring to all of us watching.

When you walked across the stage, I saw your eyes sparkle. That energy you gave off was contagious. It filled the room with an array of happiness.

We laughed with you. We clapped for you.

- Cosplayer IG(s): @folxsam
  @ohneux@pixiebutts7 and
  @mephistopheleswaifu.art, winners of Best Skit
  at Naka Kon 2019.

When you bring our favorite characters to life, it sets off a chain reaction. Those of us watching are able to access those happy memories and smile.

Think about it this way, some of us in the audience haven't smiled in weeks or even months. Life has a way of bringing you down. But you, you amazing cosplayer you. You gave me, and everyone else, a chance to just be in the moment and enjoy it.

To my Naka Kon 2019 cosplay contestants, know that I was watching you and know that you set off a joy that will show light in a darker world. Thank you so much.

Never stop what you're doing.

CHAPTER THIRTY

TOP COSPLAYS I WOULD BUILD IF I WERE TALENTED LIKE THAT

Snip, snip! Is that the sound of fabric scissors? Nope, it's an incoming slew of cosplay snippets for your enjoyment!

- Calhoun from *Wreck It Ralph* - Listen, she is one dynamite gal! I know a little of armor-smithing with foam, but my execution level is zero. I can dream though.
- Miss Frizzle from *The Magic School Bus* - While this can be done in a simple fashion, I REALLY need those light up Saturn earrings to truly complete this ensemble.
- Te Fiti from *Moana* - I always thought it would be really amazing to enter as a ball of fire, then do a twirl and you get the earthy, flowery, green Te Fiti at the end of the movie. That would be my absolute dream and I have no idea where I would start with making that.

Cosplays I Will Never Get Tired of Seeing

- Tiana from *The Princess and The Frog* - I always HAVE to get a pic with as many Tiana's as possible. I do not care how elaborate it is, if it's store bought or homemade. If you have a green dress and a frog, I'm asking you about your man catching beignets.
- Anything That Lights Up - If it lights up, I'm squealing all the way over to you.
- Baymax from *Big Hero 6* - Did I mention that *Big Hero 6* is one of my favorite Disney Movies? It may have something to do with Fall Out Boy being on the soundtrack. Anywho, I love Baymax. I actually got to hug Baymax at Disney World and he was so so soft!
- Puns, As Much as I Hate Them - oh gosh, when I get the joke, I'm laughing the whole con. I've seen people dressed as Cereal Killer (just a bunch of boxes of cereals with fake knifes in them) One Night Stand (literally just as a night stand) and so many more that left me cracking up!

What Every Cosplayer Might Randomly Need at An Event

- A Change of Shoes - I have never been one who was able to walk in heels and purposefully choose cosplays where I don't have to. But, man, at the end of the day, some cosplayers feet are pretty beat from doing all of that walking. If you have one of those foldable flats or even a

pair of house shoes, you may be able to make a
new best friend.

- Help to The Bathroom - Some costumes are
extravagant and very true to the character.
While the biggest piece of advice to survive a
con is to stay hydrated, eventually, you have to
go relieve yourself. Do you wanna do a
cosplayer a huge favor? Watch their things
while they go to the bathroom. Or even better,
help them hold up or get out of their costume
so they can pee. Heck, I needed that help with
my wedding dress and it was a major relief that
someone was willing to help me hold up that
heavy, poofy dress.

- Bobby Pins - Those cute curly hairstyles will
sweat out and wigs will start to slide.

- Tape - Things tear and props fall apart. Be a
hero to a cosplayer in need.

- Tissue - Runny makeup. Enough said.

- Ibuprofen - All that walking, a cosplayer may
need some quick pain relief that they weren't
able to store anywhere on their costume.

- An Extra Pair of Hands - Whether it's just a
second person to take the picture or hold a prop
so they can tie their shoes, cosplayers are often
overwhelmed because, well, they only have two
hands. Help someone out if you see they need it
and they will be forever grateful.

CHAPTER THIRTY-ONE

KANTCON PROVES THAT GAMING IS FOR EVERYBODY

K antCon is a tabletop convention located in Overland Park, Kansas. Every year, gaming enthusiasts get together to do what they love most: game.

From my Instagram Takeover, you could tell there were plenty of geeky vendors in the gaming halls. There was no shortage of dice holders, merch with gaming references, and D20 dice. In fact, one of those dice was a big old stuffed version that I plan to buy for me...I mean, Bby-8.

But attending a gaming convention can make you question yourself. *Am I enough of a gamer to be here? What kind of knowledge do I need to have to go in?*

The answer: None. Seriously, come as you are. What are your other excuses?

"I have kids and don't have a babysitter"

Bring them with you. Seriously. KantCon is a very family-oriented convention. There is even a Kids KantCon gaming area, where there are board games, soft lightsabers, and even a Make Your Own Mask station. I saw older children playing in the main hall with the best of them.

"Seriously, I don't know much about games"

The thing I loved about KantCon is that you could have walked in their accidentally, said "Cool, I'd like to attend, but I've never played a tabletop game before," and someone would be willing to show you how to play.

There was no gatekeeping here. Everyone here was so polite and willing to teach anyone about the world of tabletop gaming.

There was a very nice gentleman who told me everything I needed to know about Artemis. Artemis is a multiplayer, co-operative spaceship game. There was a small area set up with about four laptops and a projection screen. While also helping those in the middle of their gameplay, he even came up to me and explained how the game worked. The best being is that it would work on almost any computer system. No gaming upgrade needed. I need to review this game at a later date because he had me convinced!

"I don't live in Kansas, silly"

Okay, that's a fair excuse. However, if you don't have plans to visit that neck of the woods, I encourage you to look to see if there are any tabletop gaming conventions in your area.

Overall, I think most cons *try* to be inclusive, but KantCon really means it. Not once did I run into anyone who was like "You don't know what that is?" *scoff.* Children and adults alike were on the game floor, having an amazing time. Above all, everyone was super respectful and kind to everyone.

CHAPTER THIRTY-TWO

LIFE LESSONS LEARNED FROM FREEPLAY: A VIDEO
GAME GUIDE TO MAXIMUM EUPHORIC BLISS

Y'all know I'm a bookworm by now. I was excited to add *Freeplay* to my Goodreads list, but I wasn't expecting to get a life lesson out of it. Seriously, every page, I just sat on my couch like "Well, shit...time to make a change."

Freeplay: A Video Game Guide to Maximum Euphoric Bliss was finished in less than a day. A quick read that I assumed would go into more scientific evidence about how video games actually make you happy, ended up being one of those long car rides with your dad while he gives you a lecture about life using gaming as a metaphor.

And honestly, that is just what I needed.

Jordan Shapiro, the author, is a dad himself, so that could explain it. Shapiro actually got into gaming as an adult while playing with his children, and it brought them closer together.

And much like the good father he is, his book taught me so much about life that I really need to A) quite strongly recommend you read it for yourself, but also B) share some of his wisdom here.

Here are some of my favorite quotes from the book and how they will stick with me:

1. *"A game lost is a lesson learned."*

As a perfectionist, I needed to learn that losing wasn't the end of the world. Just like in gaming, you learn more about how to beat your bosses from losing than you do from winning.

1. *"Remember that hitting restart is not the same as giving up."*

How many times in life did I need to restart, try another level, even repeat the same level again? I felt like a failure and that I was giving up. But the thing is, I wasn't taking the whole cartridge out, I was pressing the Restart button.

1. *"Take a leap of faith. The tools you require often appear just when you need them (and not a moment before)."*

And how many times have I been too afraid to take a risk? To jump into a new relationship when I wasn't sure if I would get hurt again? To quit a toxic job because I didn't have a new one lined up just yet (and before you say anything, I found a new job two days later). This quote is the truth. I was afraid I wasn't going to be a good mom because I had never done it before. But it was a leap of faith. And I haven't looked back.

1. *"If you want to change the program - if you want to redesign the game so that it is more equal and just - you do it by paying extra attention to the design that is*

already there. Do not ignore injustice. Instead, point to it. Deconstruct it."

I was surprised that this book even spoke to the social justice. With all that's going on in the world lately, it's good to be validated that I'm fighting the good fight.

And finally, I'll leave you with this quote. it reiterates on losing, but, man, it is powerful.

1. "*Who cares whether or not you know the right way to play? Who cares if you play wrong? Losing is practicing and winning is practiced.*"

MOVIES: THE SMELL OF BURNT POPCORN AND NACHOS

CHAPTER THIRTY-THREE

QUITE POSSIBLY, MY FIRST LOVE: THE MOVIES!

Ah, the movies! While for most people movies are a way of entertainment, some of us use movies as a cheaper way to escape and travel to new worlds.

If you haven't figured this out by now, TV kind of raised me. I sat by and watched scrambled versions of Disney channel long enough to be able to watch *The Care Bears* on a weekly basis.

Movies were, and still are, a magical experience for me. It was a huge escape from real life that I craved. I owe a lot of my writing skills to watching movies. I had an understanding of how to build a plot, rising and falling action, and building an exposition before I even knew how to articulate that at all.

But most of all, movies taught me how to feel. And they taught me that so many things in life feel good. From kissing in the rain to seeing your long-lost love at the airport, movies showed me a life of one certainty. Everything will be okay in the end.

In a way, I guess the movies were sort of a first love for

me. The smell of popcorn, the collective gasping of the audience as the film reveals yet another plot twist, and the laughter, in unison, as if it were rehearsed to have perfect timing all drew me in.

I'd round the corner of an arcade (said arcade has been closed well over twenty years now) and see a roped off zig-zagged line of people standing in front of the latest movie posters. Little Quinzel loved the golden frames plastered on the walls sparkling around each movie stars smiling face. I made sure to shield my eyes from all of the horror film posters, as I had a tendency to remember every terrifying detail once I laid down to bed for the night.

While the smell of burning popcorn may be an offense to some, that smell always filled me with excitement. Seeing the smokiness of the concession stand made me feel like I was that much closer to seeing THE MOVIE.

Concessions in movie theaters are always pricey. They knew we couldn't just sit through a movie and no meal. So there ya have it. Along with a love for the movies, I also began a love for concession hot dogs and nachos. Weird, because if you handed me chips and cheese in any other setting, little Quinzel would have a fit and refuse. But something about movie theater nachos and hot dogs wrapped in foil were simply magical.

From then on, the movie theater was my escape. When I got older, I begged to be able to go with my friends. I still carry the guilt of movie-hopping at the age of thirteen. That's basically when you buy one ticket and then just keep seeing movies one after the other. I honestly couldn't tell you what I saw or what it was about because I was so wracked with guilt. I never did that again.

In fact, going from a child to a teenager, my peers found it weird that I still very much wanted to *watch* the movie. No make out sessions in the back of the theater for me, I couldn't stand to miss what was going on. The movies were having so many changes, from the quality of animation to the introduction of 3D movies, things were progressing rapidly in the movie theater world.

Early into my adulthood I thought, this is it, no more changes. Lo and behold, my movie experiences would be shaken up once more. In the middle of me enjoying my fair share of midnight premieres, for some reason I hadn't planned on seeing *The Dark Knight* early. I'm more of a fair-weather *Batman* fan, so once everyone saw it, I'd make my decision if I would go see it. It was a hot, humid night in July in my part of the world when [I refuse to mention their name] walked into a movie theater in Aurora, Colorado and killed twelve people and injured seventy more.

This shook me to my core. I never once thought of my escape to be something that should be feared. Suddenly, I found my anxiety rising every time the lights went down, nervously keeping my eyes on the nearest exist, and at times, unable to pay attention to the movie because someone was pacing in the side aisle.

Movie theaters were my safe haven, my getaway from my current life, so having someone come in and change that for me—even though I was not personally affected by it—scared the crap out of me. I even had a period of time where I felt like I was just going to wait for things to come out on DVD instead of going to the theater. I was *that* afraid.

If you've been to the blog at all, you know I've processed my issues and am hanging out in the movies more than ever. Therapy is really great y'all. I highly recommend it. But eventually I would get back to my ways and make my way to my safe space, the movie theater. At first, it was hard to sit in a theater and concentrate on a movie. I found myself focusing on the exit in the front door. I'd ask myself, *Could I get there fast enough? What if they were shooting from the exit, could I make it if I needed to go the other way, or would they just shoot me in the back?* By the time I finished running through those scenarios in my head, the movie would be over.

Repetition was key, so I kept returning, and kept coming back, until one day I realized I wasn't looking for the exit anymore. I felt safe again and it felt good.

I'm not naïve to think that the Aurora shooting couldn't happen to me. I just got to a point in my life where I wanted my safe space back. Where I didn't want to live a life where I wasn't living and just struck with fear. I assessed the risks, and I decided it was better to enjoy my life, even if it were cut short, than to live a long life afraid of going out in public.

I make it sound easy, but it's not. It took me several tries to be comfortable again. But I am so happy that I made that first step.

When I was just over the hump and enjoying the thrill of going to the movie theater, the industry would experience another hit that would be one for the history books. In late 2019, a highly contagious virus spread worldwide known as COVID-19. Millions of people were infected, thousands have even died from it. What made it so terrifying was that it changed human contact as we knew it. Social distancing was highly encouraged, if not outright enforced. What industry would be affected more than a room full of people, laughing, and sometimes crying, in a dimly lit area? That's right, the movie industry.

So when you read these upcoming movie reviews, they

will feel very dated. But what I want is for you to take the excitement that I felt in a pre-pandemic world.

Grab some popcorn and take a moment back in time with me, folks! Coming up next are some movie reviews before the world changed.

CHAPTER THIRTY-FOUR

DORA THE EXPLORER IS EVERY QUIRKY GIRL'S BEST FRIEND IN DORA AND THE LOST CITY OF GOLD

Sure, you never lived in the jungle and had a best friend named Boots. You probably never had a song about a backpack or even a cousin named Diego.

But as I kept watching *Dora and the Lost City of Gold*, I had to shake my head and say "Shoot, Dora is me." And I can bet that if you spend enough time on Geeky Girl Guide, you will feel the same way.

First of all, let me say that, next to *Aladdin*, this is one of my favorite live action remakes. Not only did they address the awkwardness of Dora breaking the 4th wall (can you say delicioso? say delicioso!) but that entire high school experience was accurate. When Diego told her that high school was life or death, it wasn't even an exaggeration. High school, in my experience, was being in survival mode all the time. Being in the jungle was probably a lot easier.

Now before I go any further, some of you may ask "why in the heck should I go see a movie about a cartoon for preschoolers?" I promise you, it's not like that at all. It's got a good plot, and it's pretty funny if you remember OG

Dora. Even if you're an adult, I think you will still enjoy it. Heck, I did!

Back to Dora. While it was hilarious that her dad told her about the dangers of raves, that piece of advice made me think. When we go to high school, none of us are prepared. All we have is tidbits of advice that we got from *High School Musical* or *She's All That*. We all go in thinking we are just going to go and be ourselves.

The scene of her dancing (doing the peacock, specifically) was enough to make me cringe with nostalgic embarrassment. I WAS that girl, I was inherently strange and getting laughed at non-stop. At the same time, I wished I had another Dora when I was in high school.

We would be weird best friends. We would sing songs and explore places and randomly yell "Swiper no swiping!" at anyone who tried to stop us.

Dora the Explorer was a fun movie. No, it won't win any Oscars, but if you're down for a fun time, and an even more fun lead character, it's a great pick me up.

CHAPTER THIRTY-FIVE

THAT SCENE YOU DON'T WANNA TALK ABOUT IN THE LION KING: LET'S TALK ABOUT IT

Nineteen-ninety-four was a good year. It was the year one of my favorite Disney movies came to theaters. I saw *The Lion King* for the first time on a humid night in June. I don't remember what I was wearing, but I am sure it was something along the lines of overalls and hair scrunchies.

I remember being amazed by "Circle of Life" and "I Just Can't Wait to Be King." My childhood was at its height when I saw Simba and Nala running through those zebras. And then...and T H E N...

I don't know exactly why I wasn't moved to tears by Mufasa's cartoon death. I was seven years old, so I had some concept of emotional intelligence, right? Well, I must not have. The older woman sitting next to me was crying-*no* -SOBBING! Full on shaking and sobbing out loud in this theater. Seven-year-old Quinzel was confused. *Mufasa's not really dead. He's in the sky, see! He wasn't going anywhere!*

Well, I definitely grew up and wasn't able to ignore the implications of death any longer. This time, not only would

I experience this remake as an adult, but as an adult who also has a child.

Because of this, I didn't stand a chance, I full on boohooed through this scene y'all.

The thing about this being live action, you see everything. You see and can feel every little detail.

Imagine watching a tiny Simba trying to avoid the stampede of animals.

When he falls from the limb, Mufasa grabs him by the nape of his neck and lovingly places him on the rock. He breathes for one second. One small second of relief before being carried away by the gazelles again.

Simba searches for him. But this time, you don't see the panic in his eyes like in the animated version. It seems like his fur sticks straight up in a panic. His body stiffens.

Mufasa emerges, using all of his strength to climb up the rock wall. He is not visibly bloody or injured, but you can tell that he climbs in pain. That it takes strength to scale this wall that he doesn't have. And then...

Betrayal, pain, and a fatal fall to the bottom. You don't need to hear him hit the ground. You don't need to find him in a pool of blood. The eerie silence aside from a single gazelle leaping, you just know.

Simba nudging Mufasa's lifeless body to wake up is enough to start the first steam of tears. But after he cries for help and nothing happens, he decides to cuddle under his dad's lifeless paw.

Say what you want about live action, I might be inclined to agree with you. But seeing this scene for R E A L about killed me.

Dooooonnnn't even get me started on "Remember Who You Are."

CHAPTER THIRTY-SIX

THERE'S A NEW PRINCESS JASMINE IN TOWN, AND SHE ISN'T HERE TO TAKE ANY OF YOUR CRAP

O ne thing you need to know about Princess Jasmine in the 2019 version of *Aladdin*, is that she IS that chick. She's not with the ish. She is not the one, or the two.

<u>And She Is the Princess You Needed All Along</u>

See, Princess Jasmine ain't the one to mess with. First of all, she's not about to sit around waiting to get married off to some man. She is not a prize to be won!

When I was a child, *Aladdin* was my favorite movie. I must have re-winded that VHS tape a thousand times. I don't even think that's an exaggeration, I can quote it forward and backward.

Princess Jasmine was a HUGE deal back in the nineties because FINALLY, SOMEONE IS BROWN! See, this was back in the day before Tiana in *The Princess and The Frog*. I took my poofy hair, tied it back in three blue hair ties, and *I. Was. It!!!*

Back then though, Princess Jasmine made me yearn for a flat stomach. But this Jasmine now? This Princess

Jasmine right *HERE??* She will make you yearn to fight for any cause that she backs.

Is she beautiful? Of-freaking-course she's beautiful, her skincare routine is ON POINT. But real talk, this is a woman who is running things. This is the woman you overlook for promotions, meanwhile, she could be running your entire company without breaking a sweat. Give. Her. All. The. Things.

On top of all that, she is watching these men in power and she is tired. *Real tired.* Because she knows that she could get it done herself and still sneak off to Agrabah later.

Jafar better watch out, because this Princess Jasmine might even throw a hand or two. But the amazing thing about her is that she wouldn't have to. She wouldn't even have to raise her voice. Just stepping into a room commands everyone present to shut up and listen. Now THAT'S power, Jafar.

Realest talk, Princess Jasmine is the kind of woman I aspire most to be.

CHAPTER THIRTY-SEVEN

USE THE BATHROOM BEFOREHAND OR IT'LL BE ENDGAME FOR YOU: MY AVENGERS ENDGAME MOVIE EXPERIENCE

O ne of the most highly anticipated movies of 2019 was, hands down, *Avengers: Endgame*. Everyone was bending over backwards to see this movie opening weekend. Geeks will be seeing it and Non-Geeks will roll their chair over to your cubicle, asking you what their children/grandchildren are so excited about. It's truly a time to let your geek side shine.

<u>If Thor Went to Movie Theaters, He Would Smash This One and Ask for More Just Like It</u>

First off, I have always thought AMC Theaters was my only choice for a movie theater because, well, that's what we got. But WOOO CHIL-AY!!! B&B Theaters were pretty on point. I love that there is so much room in the aisles!! You mean I don't have to put my whole butt in someone's face as I walk by? Yes!

This is the widest aisle I've ever seen in a movie theater. Not that you'll be getting up during the movie.

The seats were leather recliners and they were super

comfy. Comfy is what you need for a three-hour-plus movie. Can you imagine your butt and thighs fall asleep halfway through *Avengers: Endgame*? My bit of advice is that if you can splurge a little extra for nicer seating, this is the movie to do it for.

Also know that Marvel Studios spared no expense when it came to this movie, so the graphics are amazing. Splurge again on theaters that give you an even better, more immersive picture. Ours took place in the Grand Theater which had a huge screen and DTS:X sound. The sound was amazing, not like a big inaudible boom to ruin your ears for the rest of the movie. The sound was very crisp and clear.

To Pee or Not To Pee

I'm going to level with you, I knew better. I knew well ahead of time that the movie was over three hours long. I knew that I needed to pee before I left the house, which I did! But see my husband was drinking this cherry Mountain Dew and my mouth was feeling dry and then it just all went downhill from there. After the movie started, my eyes widened in a panic. "Shoot, I have to pee! When do I go?"

I got deeper into the movie and I thought to myself it's now or never. Much like the track star I was never destined to be, as soon as that movie screen was out of sight, I full on SPRINTED to the restroom, which was not close to this theater. After a quick squat and washing of hands, I sprinted back, Avengers dress flapping in the wind and the concessions workers laughing behind me.

I managed to not miss much so let me give you a piece of spoiler free advice. PEE. Become your mom and threaten yourself to go before you leave the house. Make yourself go again when you are in the theater. And no drinks. NONE. B&B Theaters is planning to sell Avengers-themed drinks for the movie and if I were you, grab your drink AFTER THE MOVIE.

Take it from someone who effed up. Give your bladder a pep talk. But if you have to pee and want to avoid missing an important moment, I would say you are good until Ant-Man is looking out of a window and smiling. Once that happens, stay in your gosh darn seat. You, and that traitor of a bladder, are in this for the long haul.

My food was delicious!

Be Kind to Your Concessions Folks

I had two of the concessions folks call me over "Excuse me," one of them said, "but we haven't seen the movie yet. Could you please tell everyone not to spoil the movie for us when they come out?"

So I took my happy ass to the theater and asked everyone to be kind to the concessions people and don't talk about what we see in front of them. And they obliged.

Just be real respectful of who you talk around guys. Yes, you're excited and yes, you wanna shout out from the rooftops, but be mindful of the people working round the clock who even make going to the movies a thing. Got it? Good!

So, Did You...Did You Like It?

In conclusion, with no spoilers attached, to answer any of your burning questions...

The answer is yes. Go see this movie.

CHAPTER THIRTY-EIGHT

STAR WARS: THE RISE OF SKYWALKER REVIEW AS TOLD BY PIXAR'S 'INSIDE OUT' CHARACTERS

So here we are! The highly anticipated *Star Wars: The Rise of Skywalker* is here and I... Well, I have a lot of feelings.

I always get nervous about posting some of the highly anticipated movie reviews. In fact, I haven't been this nervous since *Avengers: Endgame*. Seeing *Endgame* a week and a half early had me sweating bullets. What if I say something that *might* be a spoiler? Luckily, I just told you guys when the best time to go to the bathroom is, so no spoilers there.

Let's get this out of the way. There are a lot of negative reviews of *Star Wars: The Rise of Skywalker* out there but I enjoyed it! Along with that enjoyment, it made me feel a lot of feelings. With that being said, I've found the perfect way to discuss *Star Wars* without spoiling a thing for you.

Remember the movie *Inside Out*? It followed the emotional journey of eleven-year-old Riley. Joy, Anger, Disgust, Fear, and Sadness banded together to teach us the inner journey of one pre-teen's emotions.

Much like *Inside Out*, *Star Wars: The Rise of Skywalker* was an emotional roller coaster. So let me use the *Inside Out* characters to vaguely tell you how this movie made me feel.

Joy

Like I said earlier, I really loved this movie and there were many moments that had me grinning from ear to ear. I am a huge fan of Rey doing...literally anything. Many people were up in arms about having a female protagonist in *Star Wars* and I strongly disagree with them. Rey is an amazing character to watch on screen and I root for her until the end.

I've had a pretty big crush on Fin since *Star Wars: The Force Awakens*, but man, in this movie, he looks fine as hell. It's nice to watch him on screen. *swoon*

Fear

Star Wars: The Rise of Skywalker does a pretty amazing job of keeping you on your toes. There was a moment where I thought a very bad thing happened to a character I loved, and I was distraught! Everything ended up being okay, but my heart dropped when I watched that scene.

Anger

I can't go into detail on what I'm pissed at in case I spoil anything. Let's just say Fin doesn't finish what he is going to tell Rey and I am FURIOUS that it was never revealed what he was going to tell her.

Disgust

There's a quick scene where I was very much like

"They'd better not, They better NOT!... Ew! They did." That was not a ship I wanted to sail.

Some of you may have loved this. But I still say "Ew!"

Sadness

We all knew that Carrie Fisher passed away before the third movie. And we knew well before that the studio had plans to use her image in the third movie. Knowing that Carrie Fisher is no longer with us, it's a little bit of a tear-jerk to see her appear onscreen.

Bonus: Nostalgia (not an *Inside Out* character, but a very relevant emotion)

You want throwbacks to past *Star Wars* episodes? You got it! I think longtime fans will be pleased.

Overall, *Star Wars: The Rise of Skywalker* gave me all the feels in a good way. I highly recommend that you go see it!

CHAPTER THIRTY-NINE

WHAT ONCE UPON A DEADPOOL TAUGHT ME

O*nce Upon A Deadpool* arrived just in time for Christmas. As told by your favorite man-in-red, the entire plot from *Deadpool 2* is read to Fred Savage, who is duct taped to a bed.

And what, might you ask, did this Christmas-y rendition teach me?

To never EVER allow them to make *Deadpool* a PG-13 movie.

Once Upon a Deadpool might have lacked the F-word but, starting now, I'm not gonna.

First, you should know that *Once Upon a Deadpool* is literally *Deadpool 2* with, like, DVD commentary alongside Fred Savage.

I could forgive that. After all, who doesn't need more *Deadpool* in their lives? Who doesn't need a movie with a Christmas-y title that has nothing to do with the actual holiday? Let's be honest, sometimes ya just need a break.

But whoever the FUCK thought it was a good idea to sit through a *Deadpool* movie with limited cursing and blurred out asses has got to be out of their fucking mind.

Adult humor is *Deadpool*. I didn't spend my week working forty-plus-hours for a paycheck to spend it on a *Deadpool* movie with BLEEPS! You gotta be **bleep*ing* kidding me.

I am begging anyone in power. Anyone who has any hand in this. You wouldn't order a BLT and be satisfied if they left out the bacon. Don't take the bacon out of *Deadpool*. DO. NOT. EVER. make it PG-13

PG-13 *Deadpool* Sucks *bleep*. Go See It Anyway

Once you get past the bleeps, Russell telling everyone to "freak off" instead of "fuck off." and even a blurred out baby Deadpool ass, this damn movie redeems itself.

You gotta wait until the very end. The final, final end credits scene.

That's right, *Excelsior!* Right in the feels.

There's an earlier bit you should watch for. In *Deadpool 2* when Domino flies over the city in a parachute, there's a Stan Lee mural. In *Once Upon a Deadpool*, this scene happens but on the Stan Lee mural, there's a small R.I.P. on it.

Think that was it? Grab your tissues folks.

We get some funny outtakes of Stan Lee, doing his normal Marvel cameo for the film. Then he begins talking about the creation of *Deadpool*. The screen fills with images of a very happy Stan Lee.

The last thing you see before the screen fades to black?

One word: Excelsior

Now That I Can't Stop Crying. Should I See It, Quinzel?

For the final, final post-credit scene? Yes.

For the PG-13 rating? Absolutely not. I will riot if they ever do this again

What did you guys think of ~~Deadpool 2~~ *Once Upon a Deadpool*? Do you like the idea of *Deadpool* potentially being a PG-13 movie? Feel free to be wrong in the comments section below.

CHAPTER FORTY

FIVE REASONS GROWN-UPS NEED TO SEE RALPH BREAKS THE INTERNET

I got the chance to see *Ralph Breaks the Internet,* and let me tell you, it was a wang dang doodle of a good time.

If you haven't noticed, I am a full-fledged adult (I know, shocking!). And honestly I enjoyed it as much, if not more, than the kiddos.

Here's five reasons why your grown ass will love it too:

Gaming and Internet References Galore

This movie has all the gaming nostalgia that *Wreck-It Ralph* had. Now, we see references to all the things we know and love about the internet. It would be a fun game to see who can find the most logos.

Cosplay You Say?

A Geeky Girl can't really walk away from a good movie without finding a new cosplay and this one is no different. Yesss (and yes, her name is Yesss) would be the dopest cosplay ever. Yesss is actually an algorithm, dressed in all blue, hair swept to the side. Yesss dons large blue glasses, a big puffy jacket, and a fitted two-piece with blue triangles. It would be a very neat cosplay.

This Movie Passes Bechdel Test

Two women talk to each other about something other than a man. Good job, Disney!

The Cameo We All Need Right Now

There's a short cameo of a person who would really put a smile to your face. You need this cameo, trust me. Can you spot it?

Disney Princesses Steal the Show

After much controversy over Tiana's hair, we knew the Disney Princesses would be in the film. But, man, I was glad to see them in it. As someone who grew up watching these gals, it was quite amusing to see them interact with each other.

I would not be surprised if Disney sold that pajama set. I'd give it my coins.

Tiana's hair upgrade was *meh* but, whatever, at least they actually included her, amiright?

CHAPTER FORTY-ONE

THE HATE U GIVE: MOVIE REVIEW

L et's Start Here: The Book vs. The Movie
I'm going to be real with you: you will not be disappointed. Yes, there are many book-to-movie adaptations gone wrong. They will leave you confused and heartbroken.

This movie is *not* one of them.

Obviously, no movie can keep EVERYTHING from the book because, well, we would be there for six hours (not that I'd mind). However, I believe they did a great job with knowing what to cut, and new scenes staying in line with the overall focus of the book.

Kudos to you, George Tillman, Jr.

This Movie is NOT Trauma Porn

And it could have easily been. One thing I noted was the *quiet storm* that was King (why, Falcon, WHY!!). We didn't need to see him beating the almighty hell out of Seven to know that this dude was fucking it up for anyone who crossed him. You didn't even need to read the book to know that he definitely beat Seven's mom after they left.

There are MANY scenes that could have been shot just for shock value, and I'm so grateful that they went for realism instead. Don't get me wrong, you *will* need several boxes of tissues. But it's not set out to shock, disturb, or disgust you. It's set out to tell the real-life experiences that Black people face every day.

Maverick Carter is the Father We All Need in Our Lives

Russell Hornsby did a stellar job as Big Mav. I'm thinking this is going to be a separate blog post, but if you can gain anything from Big Mav, it's never judge a book by its cover.

He entered donned in tattoos (no teardrops, however) and a past that involved gangs, drugs, and imprisonment. This man was the glue that held his family together. Some things to note about him:

- In his most stressful moment, when the cops pushed him up against the glass, he never once screamed at his family.
- He encouraged Starr to "let it out" and used his traumatic experiences to give her just what she needed.
- He was always kind and affectionate to their mother, even when they disagreed.
- Think you can say that about King? ~~How about Bill Cosby?~~ *(Don't start, Quinzel!).*

I Definitely Wanted to Go 'Elevator Solange' on Hailey

I can guarantee that every black girl has gone through that level of gaslighting with a white friend. And usually confronting them on their bullshit, ends with them in tears, so you end up comforting them.

I was worried about seeing Hailey onscreen because the book version made me SOOOO angry. I read the whole "pretend like it's a piece of fried chicken, Starr" part as really aggressive. But in the movie, she had that clueless look on her face that's all too familiar. That look where you ALMOST believed that she really didn't mean any of what she said. However, both in the book and the movie, there were plenty of hints that Hailey knew exactly what she was doing, she was just really great at deflecting.

And you know what? I liked that! It gave the audience a chance to understand Starr's frustration. I also appreciate the realness of them never making up. Same as the book, but seeing it on screen was great because there are just some people who aren't gonna get it and you really do have to just move on.

Again, more realness than I expected to see onscreen. More kudos.

Sekani, Your Name Means Joy

I want you to take a close look at Sekani. And I want you to ask yourself one question.

Could you kill him?

From the start of this movie, you can clearly see why his name means joy. His bright smile and high pitched laugh were enough to make your heart melt. Watching the scene with Mav and the cops is even more painful with seeing Sekani crying. Your heart will break for this sweet little boy.

The ending, while it didn't occur in the book, was

arguably the most important scene in the movie. It brings full circle to *The Hate U Give* and what it means. Literal gasps filled the theater as Sekani pointed the gun and said: "Get away from my daddy!"

In a flash, we could see what happens next, the cops kill this poor little boy before a bullet even leaves the gun. A mother watches her son's last breath. And the news doesn't depict anything about him that we already know. They won't discuss his smile, his laughter, the fact that he still can't aim in the toilet. People will shake their heads in judgment thinking nothing of a seven-year-old's death and criticize him for holding a gun in the first place. In those short moments, the audience all saw this happening. I could even hear sobs from a rush of tears. Thankfully, Starr shielded him and none of that happened.

But my mind immediately went to Tamir Rice. That baby is no longer here.

When tragedy strikes, people deflect any way they can, often making the victim as less human as they can. So if you watched that scene and cried, you need to know that none of this is really fiction.

Don't even get me started on Lyric. If you read the book, you can understand that that poor baby saw A LOT of fucked up stuff. And what about her? How will the hate that she's given fuck everybody? That's what *The Hate U Give* is all about.

"The Hate U Give is a book, but truthfully, nothing we saw was fiction. You can't walk away from the theater with any kind of relief that this isn't our current reality.

Angie Thomas wrote the book that inspired this movie. She used her voice and it's already making a huge impact.

How will you use your voice?

CHAPTER FORTY-TWO

JUST IN TIME FOR WIZARDFEST: HARRY POTTER
QUOTES I'M REALLY DIGGING RIGHT NOW

WizardFest, a Harry Potter themed dance party that travels from city to city is just around the corner, and it's got me thinking about Harry Potter quotes that have stuck with me the most. *Swearing I'm up to no good* is a great quote for my fun life, but there are some Harry Potter quotes that have healed me like no other.

So, if you're considering going to WizardFest, or if you're wanting to throw a WizardFest in the comfort of your own reading nook, take a second to re-live these quotes with me. Feel free to use these yourself.

"It matters not what someone is born, but what they grow up to be."

"It does not do to dwell on dreams and forget to live."

"Numbing the pain for a while will make it worse when you finally feel it."

I feel kinda called out for this quote

"It is our choices, Harry, that show what we truly are, far more than our abilities."

CHAPTER FORTY-THREE

BABY QUINZEL'S TOP MOVIES

If you shake your popcorn tin and realize it's getting low, this might be a good time to head to the concession stand and get more. Don't worry, the movie snippets will be here when you get back. Don't forget to get extra butter this time.

- *Spice World* - Before you judge me, I was twelve and a HUGE fan of the Spice Girls. My absolute favorite being Baby Spice because, well, she liked all the things a twelve-year-old girly-girl likes: stuffed animals, baby doll dresses, and being inexplicably cute. The plot is...um...look we can't be good at all things, just hop in for some Spice Girl songs and join the ride.

- *Good Burger* - This is one movie that I remember smiling from beginning to end. Picture it, early 1990s and you've watched enough *Good Burger* sketches on *All That* that you are ready. See back then, when Nickelodeon released their movies on video, you knew it was good because the VHS tape was orange.

- *Land Before Time* - There's not a lot I remember about seeing this the first time. But I DO remember seeing the animation and thinking, *WOW! this looks really good*! Obviously animation has come a long way since then, but I was in such awe back then.
- *The Lion King* - The first time, it was a completely packed theater. When Mufasa died, I remember a woman's single heartbreaking sobs filling the theater. This was also one of the first movies that I saw people stand and clap at the credits.

Top Movie Quotes

- "Bury me in the ocean with my ancestors, because they knew that death was better than bondage." Killmonger, *Black Panther* - Say what you want about Killmonger, but I remember that quote just knocking the air out of me when I first saw it.
- "Tadashi is here." Baymax, *Big Hero 6* - I just wanna say I bawled after hearing that. And every time I hear it when I watch it.
- "…I cannot tell you how thankful I am for our little infinity…you gave me a forever in the numbered days, and I'm grateful." Hazel, *The Fault In Our Stars* - I'm seeing a trend where my

favorite movie quotes make me cry. By the way, I do know that this is originally a book because I have read it a million times. But I legit-sobbed at this part of the movie. It popped out for me so much seeing it on the big screen…and stabbed my heart a little bit more.

Authentically and Unapologetically Geeky

Your life begins where you can be authentically and unapologetically who you are. When you fight against it, when you try to be something other than what you are, you're going to have a bad time. Seriously, how many movies, tv shows, and after school specials is it going to take to make that point clear?

Be you, no matter how weird, no matter if you have kids, or have a chronic illness. Find the way to be authentically you each day.

I don't tell you this without the understanding of how hard it is. I was always made too loud for a world that never intended on listening to me anyway. You must understand that you won't be everyone's cup of tea. But you have to be your own cup of tea, made up just the way YOU like it.

These things we like, these things that make our hearts set on fire, the pain and struggles of it all, it's all part of the *Geeky Girl's Guide To Life.*

In the beginning of this book, I told you that I was someone you already know. But now that you've stuck it out with me until the end, you are someone I already know, too.

You are kind, you are thoughtful. You're a geek of all trades. And more importantly, you can pick up Thor's hammer.

I wholeheartedly believe that you are worthy.

QUINZEL, WHAT THE HECK ARE YOU TALKING ABOUT?

A GLOSSARY OF TERMS

Ali Barthwell - Co Founder and Social Outreach for WakandaCon. Twitter is @wtflanksteak*Ashhulee* - a cosplayer who I met at WakandaCon that was on the "Cosplay While Black" panel. Instagram handle is @ashhuhlee, so if you head over that way, you will see the amazing Max dressed as Powerline cosplay.

Baymax - The main character in the Disney movie, *Big Hero 6*. Created to be a health-conscious robot that attended to the needs of others. Also, super soft when hugged.

Bby-8 - How I affectionately refer to my nerdy child that I love so much. It's a play on the word "baby" and the droid in Star Wars known as Bb-8.

Black Panther - A Marvel movie about T'Challa, one of the Avengers, that took place in a fictional place in Africa known as Wakanda. Science is very advanced here.

BlerdCon - Taking place in good ol' Chocolate City, Washington, DC, this con is a specialized con that is all about diversity and inclusion. The term "blerd" is a mashup of the words Black and Nerd.

Brichibi Cosplays - Cosplayer known as Briana Lawrence. You can find more pics of her cosplays using the hashtag #BrichibiCosplays

Buffy The Vampire Slayer - A TV Show in the '90s that premiered on the WB. The main character Buffy Summers navigates attending high school while fighting undead monsters. And even falling in love with one.

Cards Against Humanity - A very sick and twisted card game that probably isn't the best idea to play with your conservative friends. There are black cards that ask questions and white cards that are either hilarious answers, or will have the people around you question your life choices.

Comic Con - Short for comic book convention. Most of these are held in different convention centers locally. While there are plenty of comic books at a comic con, there is always so much more in store. There are panels that cover different geeky topics such as STEM, gaming, comics, and fandom. It is a great way to get everyone in the same room talking about the same thing and a great way to meet friends. There's programming such as concerts and usually a cosplay contest. There is always a vendor hall full of goodies that you can't always get in traditional stores. There are comic cons that are more generalized and even some specialty cons for gamers, anime lovers, and even horror fans.

Console Gamer - Usually the first kind of gamer when people think of video games. This is someone who prefers to play games on a PlayStation, Xbox or any physical console that you load games into.

Cosplay - a mashup of the words "costume" and "play." It's like Halloween, but every day. Some people go the store-bought route with their costumes, and other people are super talented and can sew too. Either way, it's all for fun. Hence the word "play."

Doctor Who - I always get a kick out of explaining this show to someone who has never heard of it and are very new to the geeky world. A mad man and a blue box go traveling.

Sometimes that mad man is someone else, even a woman. No one really questions him. Oh and he has a sonic screwdriver and it does, well, a lot of stuff.

Espionage Cosmetics - a retailer that specializes in nerdy nail wraps. They also have a small makeup line and apparel as well. Check them out online at https://www.espionagecosmetics.com/.

Fall Out Boy - A band I am in love with. Four guys from Chicago get together and re-invent the term "emo." When listening to their albums, you don't know whether to laugh or to cry because it's so beautiful.

Fandom - a gathering of dorks who all like the same thing. Like an Overwatch fandom. Heck, there's probably even a spoon fandom out there.

Free Mom Hugs - an organization that dedicates itself to uplift the LGBT+ community. They attend events and give out hugs like a loving parent.

Full Elven Cosplay - Cosplayer who presented the Cosplay on the Cheap panel at Naka Kon. Their Instagram is @fullelven.cosplay.

Geek Girl Con - located in Seattle, Washington, this is an annual convention that focuses on women in science, tech, gaming, comics, and more. I haven't been yet, but this sounds like a con I need to go to. There's more info at https://geekgirlcon.com/.

Geeky Girl's Guide To Life - This lovely little blog where Leslie and I talk geek and life stuff. We don't play to a large audience, but for our small fanbase, we show out. Site is geekygirlguide.com.

Geeky Sex Toys - An Australian company that specializes in just that, sex toys. And whoever is on their writing team rocks. They have references to *Doctor Who, Deadpool, and Star Wars.* Check them out at https://geekysextoys.com/.

Icy Ace Cosplay - a cosplayer who is also a math teacher. Check out his Instagram @d.etheridge.alpha.

Inside Out - A Pixar movie that's all about emotions. Anger, Sadness, Fear, Joy, and Disgust all work together to help eleven-year-old Riley manage her emotions. Somehow this is going to work out well, right?

Jordan Sharpio - Author of *Freeplay: A Video Game Guide to Maximum Euphoric Bliss.*

Kid Fury - blogger and one of the hosts on the podcast, *The Read.* Hails from Miami and is hilarious. He will leave you in stitches. Full of (justified) rage. Oh, and if you ask for relationship advice, the answer is always "break up with him."

Krissy Victory - black cosplayer who dealt with an onslaught of racist and cringe-worthy comments after sharing pictures of her Overwatch cosplay.

Lilo and Stitch - An unbelievably cute Disney movie that takes place in Hawaii. Lilo, a young girl, runs into an alien who pretends to be a dog, so she takes him home to take care of them. And wackiness ensues. Oh, and there is also a lot of surfing, too, and that's pretty cool to watch.

Lisa Beasley - Producer and Media Relations of WakandaCon. Twitter is @lisabexperience.

Luciously_Wicked Cosplay - cosplayer who moderated WakandaCon's Cosplaying While Black Panel. Also has done an awesome Snow-oynce (Snow White/Beyonce) cosplay. Instagram handle is @Lusciously_Wicked Cosplay.

Multiple Sclerosis - an autoimmune disease that primarily attacks the coating of nerves and eventually the nerve itself. Usually requires a Disease Modifying Therapy to control the number of lesions that occur on the brain.

Naka Kon - an anime comic convention that takes place in Overland Park, KS yearly.

New York Comic Con - Another big comic book convention taking place in the opposite direction from San Diego Comic Con. This convention also has notable guests and exciting panels. Much like SDCC, the convention hall is often shoulder-to-shoulder packed with people.

Oma's Goodies - Shop selling lots of handmade goodies for baby nerds. You can find them by searching Oma's Goodies on Facebook.

Once Upon A Deadpool - Not really a third Deadpool movie, more of an extended, PG-13 version of *Deadpool 2*. It came out in theaters around Christmas time, and you know how studios are always trying to make bank around that time.

Outta Line Cosplay - cosplayer who also was a panelist at the

WakandaCon panel Cosplaying While Black. Instagram handle is @outtalinecosplay.

PC Gamer - A gamer who prefers to play on a PC. There are a lot of amazing Gaming PCs that have amazing graphics, which is one reason someone may be drawn to PC gaming. It can be a little more expensive compared to console or tabletop games, but you do get what you pay for.

Philisofher: The Love and Life of Her - a retailer who sells tees, stationery and more. Website is https://www. philosofher.com/.

Post-Partum Depression - Typically occurs after giving birth, due to the hormone fluctuations. It can be an overwhelming sadness and can last up to a year after giving birth sometimes.

Pros and Cons Cosplay - Twin cosplayers who light up the stage and take all the awards with them. Instagram is @prosandconscosplay.

Ralph Breaks The Internet - The sequel to *Wreck It Ralph* that is insanely cute.

San Diego Comic Con - The comic con that comes to mind when people talk about comic con. It's a huge convention that happens yearly in San Diego, CA and always brings in the hugest guests and biggest crowds.

Star Wars - A series of films about wars that happen among the stars…probably?

STEM - stands for Science, Technology, Engineering and Mathematics.

Sugar Bear Co - a cosplayer known as Erica Washington. Also an amazing seamstress and mental health advocate. Instagram handle is @sugabearco.

Super Dan 6488 Cosplay - cosplayer who also appeared on the WakandaCon Cosplaying While Black panel. Instagram is @danlemon88.

Sweet Tooth Confections - a lovely confectionery shop run by Ariel "Cocoa" Scott in the Chicago, IL area.

Tabletop Gamer - a gamer who plays tabletop games. There is a chance they can play Monopoly without flipping the table.

TARDIS - a Doctor Who Reference. It's a blue telephone box that The Doctor uses to time travel. TARDIS stands for Time And Relative Dimensions In Space.

Taylor Whitten - Producer and Content Strategist of WakandaCon.

The Hate U Give - A book written by Angie Thomas that recently became a movie. Both will leave you in tears, just saying.

WakandaCon - An annual comic con that takes place in Chicago, IL. While derived from the fictional land in *Black Panther*, this con celebrates diversity in an epic way. Whether you're a STEM nerd or a movie nerd, this con has something for you.

Wizardfest - inspired by Harry Potter. Wizard Fest is an event that celebrates all things Harry Potter. For reference, Harry Potter is a series of very hefty books about a boy who finds out that he's a wizard. If you grew up in a deeply religious and strict household like I did, you would realize that these books are impossible to sneak home from the library.

WonderCon - another big comic con that takes place around the state of California. This con has taken place in Anaheim, San Diego, and Los Angeles. Much like San Diego Comic Con, this con is also known for having notable celebrity guests.

ACKNOWLEDGMENTS

I have so much thankfulness and gratitude right now in this moment, reflecting on all the people who helped get this book to where it is today. First I need to thank Leslie, head geek of *Geeky Girl's Guide to Life*. None of this would be the least bit possible without you first taking the chance on me to write on a site that you built yourself. You somehow trusted me and my chaotic energy and for that, I remain forever loyal to you. I really hope you do get to meet Shownu one day.

I would like to thank the founders of WakandaCon, Lisa Beasley, Ali Barthwell, and Taylor Witten for allowing me to work press at WakandaCon and cover the most amazing convention that I've ever attended.

Thank you Sherrelle Green for not only answering my million questions at the Black Authors panel, but giving me the opportunity of a lifetime by allowing me to write this book.

I want to thank the entire team at Rose Gold Press for making this dream a reality and being just as excited about this book as I am

Most importantly, I want to thank YOU the reader, for reading this! Go forth and spread geeky goodness because it's what the world needs right now.

And lastly, I have to thank my amazing husband. My rock, my light, my comedian. If you're reading this, please dump the ice in the ice machine. Oh! And thank you for motivating me to write when I was tired, stressed, or just plain didn't want to. You believed in my dream when no one else did, and for that, I'll always make sure you have clean socks. Or buy more. Same thing.

ABOUT THE AUTHOR

Quinzel Lee is the Community and Content Manager for *Geeky Girl's Guide to Life*. Other blogs that she has written for in the past are *Don't Hate The Geek*, *She Unplugged*, and *Press Start Hub*.

While *Quinzel's Guide To Life* is her debut novel, she has always been writing. Quinzel has a Bachelor of Fine Arts degree in Theater and Creative Writing from Stephens College and has plans to write as many books and blogs as humanly possible.

Hailing from somewhere in the Midwest, she aspires to travel all over the map with her loving husband and adorably mischievous toddler

Twitter: @quinzelee
    Instagram: @GeekyGirlGuide
    Twitter: @GeekyGirlGuide
    Facebook: Geeky Girl's Guide To Life

      facebook.com/geekygirlguide
      twitter.com/QuinzeLee
      instagram.com/geekygirlguide

OURS IS A STORY THAT NEEDS TO BE TOLD

We hope you enjoyed this Rose Gold Press Special Release!

Romantic. Original. Sexy. Expressive.

Some dream in black and white, but we dream in color. Our mission is to publish quality Black romance and women's fiction novels and novellas. As a culture, ours is a story that needs to be told and this is our contribution to the many black and brown readers who have been clamoring for stories about us and for us.

To receive exclusive sneak peaks, bonus content, news about our latest releases, and sign up for our newsletter, visit us at rosegoldpress.com.

 facebook.com/rosegoldpress

 twitter.com/rose_gold_press

 instagram.com/rose_gold_press

Made in the USA
Coppell, TX
17 August 2021